Making Music

74 Creative Strategies for Electronic Music Producers

Dennis DeSantis

Ableton

Published by Ableton AG
Schönhauser Allee 6-7
10119 Berlin, Germany

First published in Germany by Ableton AG 2015

Printed by Königsdruck – Printmedien und digitale Dienste GmbH, 13407 Berlin, Germany

Printed in Germany

ISBN 978-3-9817165-0-4

Printed on PEFC-certified environmentally friendly paper.

For Alison and Cecilia,
who inspire everything I do.

Preface

What is this book?

For many artists, nothing inspires more existential terror than actually making art. The fear that we're not good enough or that we don't know enough results in untold numbers of creative crises and potential masterpieces that never get realized.

Electronic musicians used to be able to hide behind clunky, emerging technology as an excuse for inaction. But musicians today live in a golden age of tools and technology. A ninety-nine-cent smartphone app can give you the functionality of a million-dollar recording studio. A new song can be shared with the world as soon as it's finished. Tutorials for every sound design or music production technique can be found through a Google search. All of these developments have served to level the playing field for musicians, making it possible for a bedroom producer to create music at a level that used to be possible only for major-label artists.

But despite all of this, making music is still hard. Why?

Making Music was written both to answer this question and to offer ways to make it easier. It presents a systematic, concrete set of *patterns* that you can use when making music in order to move forward.

Each pattern is presented in the following way:

> A *problem* is stated. A problem is a roadblock that stops you from making progress with a particular piece of music. The problems in this book are real-world situations—you'll likely recognize many of them as things that have held you back in the past. A problem might appear at the beginning (e.g., you don't know how to start), in the middle (e.g., you've created lots of material but don't know how to organize it), or near the end (e.g., you keep making changes and can't decide how to finish).

> The problem is explained in more detail via examples and (sometimes) references to other patterns.

> A *solution* is provided. A solution is a concrete instruction or small set of instructions that will solve the stated problem. Like the problems, the solutions are also real; if you apply the solution, the problem will be solved. Note that this requires you to actually do the solution; in most cases, reading it won't be enough to move you forward. *Making Music* can show you the way, but you still need to do the work.

> The solution is explained in more detail via examples and (sometimes) references to other patterns.

Who is this book for?

If you make original music using computers and you've ever found yourself struggling to complete your musical projects, *Making Music* was written for you. While many of the patterns discussed here can probably be modified or directly applied to other types of music-making (such as composing for rock bands or string quartets), the goal of this book is to solve the specific problems that people have when working with machines, rather than with instruments or other people.

While no prior skills are really necessary to make use of this book, I've written it assuming you have a basic understanding of at least one digital audio workstation (DAW) or similar music production environment. No specific tool is required, and the problems and solutions discussed aren't specific to the workflow of any particular piece of technology. A basic understanding of the fundamentals of music—chords, scales, and concepts of rhythm—is useful but not a prerequisite.

Although it may not always be obvious, the patterns are all general enough that they can be used by musicians working with any genre of electronic music, from commercial dance music to the avant-garde. Although some of the explanations used refer to actual genres or even specific examples of music, I encourage you to read "around" these descriptions in order to get at the essence of the pattern so that you can apply it to your own work.

Who's the author?

I am a musician with a background in a variety of different worlds. I studied classical composition, music theory, and percussion, although these days I primarily write electronic music in the direction of house and techno. I grew up just outside of Detroit, and all of the amazing music that came from and through that city was a big influence in my early musical development. Although this book aims to be as genre-neutral as possible, it's very much written from my personal perspective—the things I talk about here are a reflection of things I actually think about and employ in my own music.

How to use this book

Think of *Making Music* as something like a travel guide. There's no explicit order to the patterns, although things tend to be loosely grouped by concept. You can read and experiment with the various patterns as you need them in order to solve particular problems as they come up in your own work. Sometimes the patterns will explicitly relate to others, and I often refer to other patterns to help clarify the current one. So while it's not necessary to read the whole book cover to cover, doing so will probably help you to find relationships between the various patterns and to see them as a *system*, rather than as isolated examples.

How this book is organized

The patterns themselves are grouped into sections based on where in the writing process a particular musical problem is likely to occur. These are:

> Problems of *beginning*. These are problems that prevent you from starting at all. They include problems of inspiration, problems realizing the sounds you hear in your head, etc. The solutions include exercises to develop better active listening and explorations of various ways of playing with sound, harmony, melody, rhythm, and musical form.

> Problems of *progressing*. These are the most common roadblocks when working and occur once you've made something but are still a long way from the end. They include problems of fatigue, problems developing and varying material, etc. The solutions include exercises to generate new material, shape song structure, and stay in the creative flow.

> Problems of *finishing*. These problems occur when you feel that almost (but not quite) everything is in place, but you are unable to reach a satisfactory conclusion. The solutions include ideas for creating convincing arrangements and for creating powerful endings.

Why is this book needed?

There are already many ways—books, classes, video tutorials, software documentation, private teachers—to learn about music technology and music production. I'm a strong supporter of all of this, and I encourage anyone who's interested in this book to also take advantage of these resources. But almost all of them focus on the second half of the equation—technology or production—rather than the first half: music. *Making Music* is an attempt to help people who are comfortable with the basics of music production at a technical level but who still find music-making to be a difficult process (which I suspect is all of us!).

Finally...

This book will not teach you how to use a compressor, program a synthesizer, or make a great-sounding kick drum. Those aspects of music-making are already well covered. What it will teach you is how to make music using those tools, with a specific emphasis on solving musical problems, making progress, and (most importantly) finishing what you start.

While I hope you find *Making Music* inspiring, I hope even more that what inspires you is the music you make using these patterns. *Making Music* is not a collection of vague aphorisms. Instead, it combines motivational ideas about the philosophy and psychology of music-making with hands-on tools and techniques that musicians of all kinds can use to really get work done.

Contents

Problems of Progressing

Problems of Finishing

Problems of Beginning

Three Ways to Start

Problem:

You're staring into the void of a new empty project in your DAW, and you have absolutely no idea how to begin.

The blank slate might be the most intimidating place in a creative environment. Once we're in a flow, ideas tend to spawn additional ideas. But before we have anything, all options are available, so choosing seems impossible. One Part at a Time (page 54) is certainly a way to move forward, but which one part comes first? When you have nothing, even choosing one part can feel like an impossible hurdle.

The simple-sounding answer is "It doesn't matter how you start; just do!" This might work well as a sports slogan, but it's perhaps too glib and dismissive to be really practical for creative work, in which the number of things to potentially "just do" are limitless and the path forward is not at all obvious. Here are three practical suggestions for how to begin from nothing.

Solution:

1. **Start with the foundation.** In most genres, we can think of the "bottom" of the music as being the low-pitched or purely rhythmic instruments, such as the bass and drums. On top of these are added instruments that are progressively higher in pitch. By starting with the bottom, we provide both a conceptual and musical foundation for everything else. The drums often provide the essential timekeeping elements, while the bass often provides the notes that define and anchor the chord progression. If you're working in more experimental genres that don't use these conventional instruments, it's still likely that some elements can be considered foundational—perhaps a droning layer or something that approaches a repetitive rhythm.

2. **Start with what you hear.** Many musicians never (or rarely) get spontaneous musical ideas—all of their music comes from active work. If you happen to be lucky enough to hear original musical ideas in your head, then you should absolutely use them as the basis for your own work. For example, maybe you have a melodic idea that you've been humming, or a rhythm that you've tapped out on the table. Just because these ideas came to you outside of your active music-making context doesn't mean you should discard them. On the contrary, these accidental ideas are sometimes the most interesting ones you can have.

3. **Start with what you know.** If you play a "real" physical instrument, try using it to generate your ideas. Even if you're writing purely electronic music and have no plans to use instrument recordings in your work, your natural physical connection to your instrument may help you come up with more interesting and organic musical ideas than you can get from just working with a mouse and a MIDI controller. For example, guitarists tend to voice chords and approach harmony in a different way from keyboardists. But because keyboards are the de facto control surface for entering music into a DAW, many guitarists might never think to use their guitars in an electronic music context. Drummers rarely play the kind of beats that are used

in many types of electronic music, but sitting behind a real drum kit might stimulate creative ideas that would feel alien on a pad controller. The trick with this approach is being able to accurately translate the acoustic idea to the electronic medium, but that's a good problem to have; much better than having no ideas at all.

Catalog of Attributes

Problem:

Creative musicians find inspiration in other music. While we seek to make music that is uniquely our own, every other piece of music we hear is automatically processed and becomes an unconscious part of our musical vocabulary. Taking too much is theft. Taking too little fails to acknowledge our influences.

For musicians who aim to find and develop a unique voice, there will always be an internal conflict to resolve when hearing music that is inspiring. To truly be original, is it necessary to ignore all external influence? How much can you "take" from other music before what you've made no longer feels like it's yours? What and where is the boundary between homage/inspiration and plagiarism/copying?

Unfortunately, these aren't questions with "right" answers. Objective legal issues aside, each artist needs to determine their own level of comfort when borrowing from other sources. But there are some strategies that let you infuse your own work with the "essence" of your inspiration, while simultaneously forcing you to make something new. One of these is to write a catalog of attributes.

Solution:

Listen carefully—and many times—to the piece that inspires you (the "source"). Study it, element by element and layer by layer, until you can write down a catalog of its attributes. Once the catalog feels complete, set aside the original source, instead referring only to the catalog as a template for your own new work (the "target").

Consider the attributes of sound, harmony, melody, rhythm, and form. Write something concrete about what you hear for each attribute. If you're comfortable with notation, feel free to use it in your catalog, but sparingly; the goal is to capture only the framework or scaffolding of the source, including the aspects that make it inspiring, but without simply recreating it. You should end up with a description, not a transcription.

The catalog's level of detail may vary depending on a variety of factors: your own ability to translate what you hear into words, the depth and complexity of the source, the amount of time you choose to spend, etc. What is important is not the actual level of specificity, but only that it gives you enough to use as a template without having to refer to the original again during your own creation process.

A basic catalog of attributes might look like this:

> 122 bpm

> Sound elements: drums, (808, four-on-the-floor, lots of filter motion on closed hats), bass line (FM-ish?), electric piano (distorted but dry), female vocals (breathy verses, full-voice choruses), lead synth (big supersaw, but only after the second chorus).

> Harmony: mostly D minor alternating with A major until breakdown. Breakdown section is in D major (sort of?). After breakdown, rest of track is in E minor alternating with B major.

> Melody: not much. Lots of D, with occasional jumps up to A and down to B♭.

> Rhythm: four-on-the-floor drums (basic house beat). Bass line is

mostly offbeat eighth notes (trance influence?). Cool metallic hit on the "and" of beat 2 every four bars.

> Form: additive layering; drums start, then each element enters one by one. At breakdown, everything drops out except hi-hats and bass line, then rebuilds additively. Form is all 16- and 32-bar sections. (Verse 16, Verse 16, Chorus 16, Breakdown 32, Chorus 16, Chorus 16)

This catalog of attributes could describe an endless number of new works. In fact, you can probably hear music that fits these attributes in your head already. It is complete enough to serve as a template but not so descriptive as to allow for a recreation of any particular piece of existing music; if two musicians read the catalog, there would be almost no possibility that they would use it to write the same thing. Now try to put yourself in the mindset of one of those musicians; using only the catalog as a recipe, make something new.

Avoidance List

Problem:

Sometimes when we listen back to a recently finished track, we find that it's too similar to something we've written before. We've managed to develop a personal style, but we're so bound by it that we feel unable to create things that really feel new.

We often discover this after listening back to a track a few days after it's finished. While working (or immediately after), we don't notice the similarities. But when we have a bit of distance from the new work, we're suddenly able to hear how it compares to the rest of the music we've done, and the similarities become painfully obvious. Often, it's a similarity in sound—the same types of samples or synth sounds keep coming up. Sometimes, it's a similarity in form—we rely on the same kinds of transitions or formal structures from track to track. It can feel like you're writing the same music over and over again.

Note that, depending on the genre you're working in, a high degree of consistency may be exactly what you're going for. In commercial styles like EDM, for example, predictability of structure and overall sound is a fundamental attribute of the style. Radical sound design and unusual forms wouldn't make sense in this music, and the interest comes from seeing how effectively artists can work within the strict boundaries that define the genre.

But if you're uncomfortable with the feeling that you're stuck on repeat, here's a potential solution.

Solution:

As soon as you realize that a new track is too similar to something you've done before, start writing a list of the specific musical attributes that make you feel this way. Carefully analyze all of the potential categories—sound, harmony, melody, rhythm, and form—and write down the specific technique that's been repeated. This will form an "avoidance list" for your next track, a list of things that you've decided ahead of time to *not* do.

If you're feeling inspired, try to come up with some alternatives to the attributes you'll avoid. This can serve two purposes: First, it gives you something to actually do, which will save time when you're working on the track. But more importantly, it might help you identify why you've been relying on a particular type of technique in the past. For example, if you've forbidden yourself from using tempo-synced dub delays, you might decide to experiment more with reverb. But perhaps the underlying reason for your use of delays in the first place is that you're uncomfortable with the idea of space and silence in your music. Maybe this problem can be solved by adding additional layers of musical material. Or maybe there isn't really a problem to solve, and your next track could make interesting use of silence that you would normally have simply filled in by force of habit.

You can think of the avoidance list as a kind of negative version of the Catalog of Attributes (page 22). The goal here is to find patterns in existing music that should be avoided, rather than emulated. The difference, of course, is that you're analyzing attributes in your own work rather than that of another artist.

An avoidance list might look like this:

> stay away from 123-127 bpm; try faster (or maybe slower?)

> no 808 samples; (try FM drums or processed acoustic samples)

> no "wood" sounds; (find different percussion elements—white noise or metal?)

> no (or less) filter cutoff/resonance sweeps; (try FM for timbral changes)

> no (or less) sidechaining; (write a bass pattern that avoids the kick, rather than relying on ducking)

> stop using only two chords; (spend time really working out a more comprehensive progression)

> no auto-tuned/chopped vocals (another organic source? non-pitched spoken word samples?)

> no drum-less breakdown; (find another way to create formal tension and release)

Now as you start a new track, you're forced to find new strategies rather than relying on techniques that you already know you're tired of hearing. You may find it difficult to work without these reliable elements of your vocabulary in place. But looking for alternatives will help you expand that vocabulary, while simultaneously ensuring that this track won't simply be a clone of the last one.

~ A note of caution: As with Arbitrary Constraints (page 42) and Process vs. Product (page 108), you should feel free to abandon your pre-planned restrictions at any point in the writing process. If you find that you've eliminated techniques that really would sound better in the context of the music you're working on, you should absolutely allow yourself to use them. Restrictions, plans, and structure can be important learning tools and can help you to get out of ruts. But in every case, the most important thing is the song, and you should do whatever will make the best song possible, including deviating from the plan if necessary.

Active Listening

Problem:

Although you listen to a lot of music, you don't really have a sense that you're learning from what you listen to. You know what you like, but you don't really understand why you like it or how to extract compositional or technical ideas from what you hear so that you can reuse them in your own music.

For most people, listening to music is a passive experience. We turn music on but then engage in another primary activity. The music is playing, and we're loosely aware of it, but it's serving a decorative or soundtrack-like purpose for whatever else we're doing. Although this is certainly better than not listening to music at all, you can learn more if you spend at least some time engaged in *active listening*.

Solution:

Active listening simply means listening as the primary activity, and it's an important skill to develop. Rather than using music as the background for another activity, try listening without doing anything else. This requires time, quiet, and focus, which are skills you need for your own production work anyway. A good way to start is by just putting on some music and then turning your attention to it entirely. If you're listening at your computer, close any open applications (and, ideally, your eyes as well). At this point, you're not trying to listen with a *particular* focus, but rather a *general* one. If you can concentrate and avoid distraction, you'll be amazed by how much more you hear than in a passive listening state.

The next step in active listening is to start trying to deconstruct what's happening in the music you're listening to. Here are some tips for doing this:

Listen in Layers

A great way to actively listen is to listen to the same piece multiple times and force yourself to focus on a different specific parameter each time. For example, spend one pass listening only for:

Sound*:* What are the timbral characteristics of this music? What instruments are used? What is the texture (dense vs. sparse)? Are there some specific production techniques that you recognize (either from your own or other music)? What kind of acoustic "space" is suggested by the music (dry vs. reverberant, near vs. far, etc.)?

Harmony*:* What key (if any) is the song in? What chords are used? Is there a chord progression that happens throughout, or does it change from section to section? If there are no overt chords (as in some minimal or experimental music), is harmony implied in another way?

Melody*:* What's happening in the melody? Does it have a wide or narrow range? What is its general contour: Angular, with lots of leaps? Stepwise, with motion mostly by one or two semitones? What instrument or voice has the melody? Does this ever change? If there is no overt melody (as in some minimal or experimental music), is melody implied in another way?

Rhythm: How are events distributed within short time ranges like a bar or phrase? Are there patterns that repeat, or do rhythmic gestures happen only once? Are rhythms and tempo overtly identifiable, or is the music free and largely arrhythmic? What instruments have the most impact on the rhythm? What do the less rhythmic instruments do?

Form: How does the song evolve over time? Are there clear sectional divisions or are there Fuzzy Boundaries (page 124) between regions? What defines one section versus another? Do certain instruments play only in some sections or is the instrumentation the same in every section?

Additionally, if there are specific instrumental or vocal parts that you'd like to understand better, try spending an entire listening pass focusing entirely on only one part. For example, the best way to learn how the bass line works in a particular song is to tune out everything else and focus just on the bass line.

Listen in Chunks

By isolating and looping short durations of music, you can more easily focus on the specific parameters or instruments discussed earlier. The best tool for this is your DAW. Try loading the song you want to listen to into your DAW's timeline, adjust the project tempo to match the song, and then set the loop to a short region—one or two bars or, at most, a single musical phrase. Listen to this loop as many times as necessary in order to really hear what's happening in the parameter you're listening for. Then advance to the next chunk and repeat. When you're done, go back to the beginning and gradually expand the loop length so that you're covering a larger amount of time in a single listening pass. Listening in chunks like this is also a great way to learn or memorize a particular part by ear.

Listen Subjectively

In addition to helping you learn how a particular piece of music "works," active listening can also help you understand your subjective responses to music. For example, are there particular aspects of the song that sound familiar, nostalgic, emotional, etc.? Can you explain why (perhaps with reference to the parameters discussed earlier)? When listening passively, it's common to have some kind of emotional response. But via active listening, you have a chance to understand what it is, specifically, that causes that response. And once you understand a technique or musical gesture, you'll be able to adapt it for use in your own music.

Listening to Music You Hate

Problem:

Although you listen to a lot of music, you tend to listen within a specific set of genres. And you pretty much exclusively listen to music that you like, or at least music that you expect you'll like based on your previous experience, recommendations, etc.

Even if you write exclusively in a single genre, you owe it to yourself to spend some time listening to a wide variety of music. Here are some tips for how (and why) to listen to music that you may not enjoy.

Solution:

Most people listen to music for entertainment. But producers and composers owe it to themselves to also listen in order to *learn something*. Inevitably, this will mean spending at least some time listening outside of your comfort zone, to music that you don't like.

This is more than just listening to genres that are closely related to what you normally listen to. For example, if you consider yourself primarily a techno producer, don't be too proud of yourself if you occasionally listen to house music. It's critical that you expand your range of listening to genres that you would never normally listen to for pleasure.

Why is this important? As you listen, consider the following questions:

Are there musical techniques you can use?

If you write in only one genre (and especially if you listen to only one genre), perhaps you've developed a set of working techniques that's fairly consistent and "appropriate" for the kind of music you make. This may work for you, but it also exposes you to the risk of writing the same music over and over. Other types of music may be made in entirely different ways, and perhaps there are techniques from those worlds that you can appropriate for your own use.

As an example, consider opera (a genre that many electronic producers probably don't spend a lot of time listening to). A single opera may last for hours—a time scale that's closer to an entire DJ set than a single track. How does tension and release work over this amount of time? How does form work? What about harmony? Rhythm? Melody? Overall sound?

Are there production techniques you can use?

In addition to musical techniques, there is also a huge amount you can learn about production when listening to other genres.

Consider country music, for example. Whatever you might think of this music as entertainment, there is no doubt that contemporary country music is generally extremely well-produced and borrows a lot of mixing and production concepts from contemporary pop music. But there are some significant differences. For example, vocals in country music are often much louder than vocals in pop music (or in electronic genres with vocals). Also, pop music (and many electronic genres) tends to be quite bass-heavy, while country tends to emphasize guitars and other mid-range instruments.

Whether or not those production characteristics are useful in your own music depends on what you're trying to accomplish. But simply being aware of what's happening in a wide variety of styles might inspire your creativity or shake you out of your own stylistic ruts.

Why do people like this?

No matter what you're listening to, and no matter how terrible you think it is, someone out there loves it. And unless you're writing music exclusively for yourself, it's a useful intellectual exercise to try to understand why people like what they do. There are, of course, social pressures; people like things because they're popular, or because their friends like them, or because they represent a recognized signifier for a particular subculture. But there are also genuine musical preferences which vary widely (and wildly) between people. Even if you have no intention of writing music for the opera or country music fan, thinking about how other music works, and why disparate groups of people like what they do, can help you become a more well-rounded musician, which can only improve your music.

Mise en Place

Problem:

Getting into a creative mindset is hard enough, but once you're in it, something inevitably goes wrong. DAWs crash, plug-ins need to be updated, you're missing samples you absolutely need, you're out of coffee, the dog needs to be walked, etc. And once you've fixed all of the problems, huge amounts of time have gone by and your creative impulse is gone.

There are many things that can impede progress in the studio. Some of these things are legitimate issues (like equipment that suddenly fails), while others are distractions that we're able to convince ourselves are important enough to get in our way (like a new email).

But because the creative impulse is so fleeting, it's vital that we're able to actually get music made when ideas come. This means making sure that everything we'll need to work is set up and ready to go beforehand, so that we can focus when we need to. Here are some ideas.

Solution:

The term *mise en place* (roughly translated from French as "put in place") comes from the culinary world and refers to the careful preparation that goes into setting the physical (and mental) space prior to the actual work of cooking. This means making sure that the tools and ingredients you'll need are easily at hand, the kitchen is clean and safe for use, and you've thought ahead to the end of the recipe to ensure that nothing unexpected will stop you once you've started.

There are clear parallels between work in the kitchen and work in the studio, and employing mise en place as part of your music-making process can help you stay focused when inspiration strikes.

Prepare Your Ingredients

Are your DAWs and plug-ins up to date? Do you have the samples you need? Are they named and organized in such a way that you can find them without needing to go on a time-consuming (and inspiration-destroying) search through all of your hard drives? Just as importantly, are the samples you *don't* need out of your way and easy to avoid? Are your controllers, audio interface, headphones, and speakers connected and working? Does any hardware need drivers? If you're using external instruments like synthesizers or effects, are they patched in and turned on? If you're using acoustic instruments like drums, are the mics set up and working?

Prepare Your Workspace

Is your chair comfortable? Is your desk uncluttered? Can you physically access any necessary hardware? If you're collaborating with other people, are they plugged in and ready to make noise? Are they comfortable and also in a creative mindset?

Prepare Yourself

Are you hungry or thirsty? How about any animals or children you're responsible for? Is there a critical phone call you need to make or email you need to send? Are your neighbors or roommates going to be bothered by the sound you make?

Nothing kills the creative flow more than having to stop and solve a non-creative problem. Making sure that these factors are dealt with ahead of time means that you're able to fully embrace the music-making process, with less risk of distraction.

In addition to employing mise en place prior to starting work, there are some additional kinds of preparation and organization actions you can take that will help you be ready when inspiration strikes:

Make Templates

If you find that there are particular combinations of instruments or sounds that you're using often, save empty template projects with those instruments already loaded so that you can be ready to start creating as soon as you have an idea. For example, if you switch between your own solo work and working with other musicians, save a template for each scenario rather than rebuilding these environments from your DAW's default project over and over again. The goal is to get from idea to actual creation as quickly and effortlessly as possible.

Organize as You Go

Even a well-prepared environment can quickly fall into chaos during the heat of the creative moment. As you're working, try to stay as organized as you can (but without falling out of music-making). For example, name tracks before you record onto them, both so you can see at a glance what you're working on, and also so newly created clips on those tracks "inherit" useful names. If your DAW allows it, use color to create visual associations between related clips or tracks. And throw away anything that you've definitely decided not to use. Removing clutter from your project helps you to focus on the important things that remain (and may also reduce your CPU load or memory usage).

Always Be Ready to Capture

Great ideas might come to you when you're outside of the studio. Ideally, you're always prepared with a field recorder or a smartphone app to quickly capture interesting sounds, or even melodic or rhythmic ideas that you can hum or sing before you forget them. You can even use a notebook to capture ideas—in musical notation or in text, pictures, or any other system that will allow you to remember it. The important thing is that you have these capturing tools with you at all times.

Although mise en place can be a huge productivity boost, make sure that you find time for this preparation work that is not the same as your creative time. Don't start getting organized when you're actually inspired to make music. If you feel like making music, that should always take priority. It's much harder to find the energy to be creative than it is to find energy for mise en place, which you can make yourself do anytime. And it's much better to act quickly on a creative impulse—even if you're completely unprepared—than it is to postpone it, try to get organized, and then find you've lost your motivation. Use the time when you're *not* inspired to take care of mise en place.

Arbitrary Constraints

"My freedom thus consists in my moving about within the narrow frame that I have assigned to myself for each one of my undertakings. I shall go even further: my freedom will be so much the greater and more meaningful the more narrowly I limit my field of action and the more I surround myself with obstacles. Whatever diminishes constraint diminishes strength. The more constraints one imposes, the more one frees oneself of the claims that shackle the spirit."
— Igor Stravinsky, *Poetics of Music*

Problem:

Music production with a computer offers a limitless field of possibilities. Any sound can be made, manipulated, re-recorded, re-manipulated, etc. But while an infinite range of options might sound appealing, it also means that decision making is hard. The more options you see, the more you need to make active choices about which ones to pursue and which ones to ignore.

Limiting the field of possibilities isn't just about making it easier to work. It's also about making it possible to begin at all. If every possible starting direction is equally appealing, how could you ever choose one?

Solution:

Apply arbitrary constraints before starting to work. Create a "narrow frame" of possibilities, and then act entirely within that frame. Applying arbitrary constraints helps to limit your field of options, allowing you to move forward.

It's important to note that these constraints really are arbitrary; you're attempting to eliminate *perfectly valid* options rather than *bad* ones. Bad options are easy to deal with; your own musical sensibilities will reject them automatically. But valid options need special care because their validity requires you to make active choices about whether to pursue or reject them. Eliminating them arbitrarily helps you avoid decision paralysis. Also, the fact that the constraints are arbitrary means that it doesn't really matter if you're wrong. If you realize during the course of your work that you've constrained yourself too much, or in the wrong direction, you can simply choose to remove the constraint.

Here are a number of ideas for arbitrary constraints, both related to the music itself and also to working method:

Musical Constraints

> **Make every sound from one sample.** An extreme restriction on available sound sources forces you to really think about the character and possibilities of the sounds you choose. Can you make a kick drum sample into a lush pad? How about a hi-hat? What kinds of processing could you use for these transformations?

> **Completely avoid an instrument that would be expected in the genre.** For example, the untitled Peter Gabriel album commonly called *Melt* has no cymbals. Prince's classic song "When Doves Cry" has no bass line. These kinds of restrictions force your decision making process into new directions. If an entire functional role is missing, how do you fill the gap? In the case of *Melt*, Gabriel had to find ways to propel time forward without relying on mainstays like hi-hats or ride cymbals. His solution was a range of unconventional

percussion instruments. In the case of "When Doves Cry," Prince chooses to leave the sonic space unfilled. Consider both options in your own work.

Constraints on Time

> **Give yourself a deadline.** Nothing motivates like a due date. Since work always expands to fill the available time, it's necessary to actually put a limit on that time. If you find self-imposed deadlines to be too "soft," try having someone else assign the deadline for you, with the requirement that you show them the work at the end to ensure accountability. Or engage in a collective challenge, such as February Album Writing Month.*

> **Schedule tasks as if they were appointments with yourself.** Try using a calendar to restrict specific types of work to specific times. For example:
Sound design: 7-8pm
Form/song structure: 8-9pm
Mixing: 9-10pm

Timeboxing (page 82) specific tasks serves two purposes: It forces you to narrow your focus while simultaneously eliminating the risk of non-musical distractions (Facebook, etc.). You wouldn't check your email in the middle of a business meeting, so treat these "appointments" with the same kind of care.

* http://fawm.org/

Constraints on Space

> **Change your venue.** If you're used to making music in a particular place, try moving to a different one. Simply moving from your bedroom studio to the local coffee shop forces your hand in a number of ways. First of all, you're limited by what you can take with you—no racks of external hardware, for example. Secondly, you're in an environment that is at least somewhat unfamiliar, so you're unable to fully relax (and thus become distracted). Many musicians avoid having a home studio altogether, instead choosing to rent studio space so that they can separate their working mindset from their living mindset.

Although you may not realize it at first, you're most likely already applying certain constraints to your work. For example, simply making the choice to work within a specific genre already eliminates a huge range of musical possibilities. To say that you're working on a "house track" as opposed to a "Balkan folktronica track" implies that you understand certain general characteristics (the instrumentation, rhythms, and harmonic language that identify a given piece of music as being "in" a particular genre) that describe one music as opposed to another.

“Write drunk; edit sober”

Problem:

Sometimes during music-making, we find moments of amazing creativity and flow. But because we have in mind the ultimate end goal of “a great track,” we sometimes stop mid-flow to edit, correct, or otherwise disrupt the creation process. And once we do, it can be difficult to get back into the flow.

Creativity is an intrinsically messy and uninhibited process. Editing, on the other hand, is about refinement and order. “Write drunk; edit sober”—a quote often attributed (most likely incorrectly) to author Ernest Hemingway—uses drunkenness versus sobriety as a metaphor about levels of self-control and the importance of working both with and without restraint. Both modes of working are necessary to create something good, but problems can arise when we don’t keep a clear division between the two. Allowing them to overlap runs the risk of breaking our creative flow.

Solution:

Force yourself to compartmentalize your work into two discrete phases. During the *creation phase*, your goal should be to capture as much material as possible. Only move forward in time. Delete nothing. Once you've recorded something, consider it finished. Better yet, forget about it entirely and move on to the next thing. Aim for speed and quantity, judge nothing, and be prepared to make lots of mistakes.

Once you've captured a lot of material (maybe after a set amount of time, or simply once you get bored) switch to the *editing phase*. Now, your goal is to carefully refine the material that you generated during the creation phase. Resist the urge to generate anything new during this process, and instead ruthlessly delete, trim, reorder, or otherwise curate the material you made earlier. It's likely that you'll throw away the majority of what you made, and this is healthy. Most of what we make in a truly judgment-free creation mindset is likely to be terrible.

A side benefit of working so freely during the creation phase is that you may find things during the *editing* phase that are actually amazing but are unusable within the context of the project you're currently working on. When that happens, just save the material that's worth saving (but is wrong for the current song) into a "scraps" folder (see Scraps and Sketches (page 94)). Then the next time you're beginning a new track but aren't in the mood to start from scratch, simply pull something interesting out of your scraps folder. Depending on how developed your scraps are, you might be able to pick one up and move directly into a new editing phase.

A good technical approach to working during the creation phase is to always be recording. Even if you're just improvising at the keyboard and have no plan or direction, be sure to capture every note you play. A common working method for electronic musicians is to use the DAW as the recording device but use hardware or other sources outside of the computer to generate sound. A collection of synthesizers generating MIDI and/or audio lets you get your hands on something that doesn't feel like an editing environment, allowing you to step away from the DAW (and its inherent bias towards editing). Press record, then play and tweak knobs, capturing everything you do as a kind of free-form jam. While jamming, try to forget that you're recording. Don't try to make something perfect. Simply indulge in the uninhibited freedom of exploring sound. Follow your instincts—if something is working, let that lead you in a direction. If something isn't working, abandon it, but do so *without* stopping the recording. The trick is to stay out of judgment mode as much as possible. Simply capture as much as you can, following your instinctive sense of what's right. Don't worry about hard drive space. If you really need to reclaim the space, you can do that later during the editing phase.

Even if you work entirely in the computer, try to find some working methods that are somehow analogous to this physical division between instruments and editors. For example, maybe use one DAW as your creation space and another as your editing space. By treating these as distinct virtual environments, it may be easier to switch between the two modes of working. Alternatively, find a collection of instruments and effects that allow you to create lots of material in an evolving, organic, connected way. For example, modular synthesizers and arpeggiators, even virtual ones, can be great sources of material during the creation phase. Start your recording even before you've started building a modular patch, so that you can catch any happy accidents that occur on the way.

If your DAW allows for comprehensive routing options between tracks, try capturing both MIDI and audio simultaneously during the creation phase. This will give you more ways to edit later and provide more raw fodder for refinement. It will also save time in the editing process because you don't have to listen to everything twice—the MIDI and audio will contain analogous information, so you can listen through a single pass and then decide whether to rework the MIDI, the audio, or both.

The balance between play (creation) and work (editing) is necessary to generate good results. Like Subtractive Arranging (page 300), this approach works because it allows you to remove rather than create, and it's much easier to decide that something is bad once it exists than it is to make something good from nothing. It saves you from having to make the "right" thing the first time, when you may be struggling to simply make anything at all.

~ Note: I wrote the first draft of this chapter in a text editor with an option called "Hemingway Mode," which disables the Delete key. At the end of the creation phase, it was nearly 2000 words long. After editing, it's about half that, and the paragraphs are almost completely reordered.

Choosing a Tempo

Problem:

You're often not sure how to choose the right tempo for a track in progress. Does it really make a difference if your track is at 124 bpm rather than 125, for example? And why do some ranges of tempos seem to allow for much more musical flexibility than others?

The choice of tempo depends on a variety of factors, including intended genre, intended audience, and (above all) personal preference. Here are some thoughts about tempo.

Solution:

If you already have a clear intention to write in a specific, well-established genre, then the range of "acceptable" tempos is probably already decided for you; tempo is one of the defining characteristics of genre. Here is a list of common tempo ranges for a number of electronic genres:

> Dub: 60-90 bpm
> Hip-hop: 60-100 bpm
> Downtempo: 90-120 bpm
> House: 115-130 bpm
> Techno/trance: 120-140 bpm
> Dubstep: 135-145 bpm
> Drum and bass: 160-180 bpm

Note that anything genre-related is not an exact science, and for each of these genres there are likely to be many exceptions and outliers. But as a general rule, if you're deliberately working in one of these genres, choosing a tempo within these ranges should work.

So how do you decide on a more specific tempo? This is largely dependent on personal preference and musical context. Start with something in the middle of the range, but then try occasionally changing the tempo while working on the track and see if something just feels "right." You can also try some of the techniques suggested in Deliberately Bad Listening (page 286) to see how the tempo feels in unusual monitoring contexts. Sometimes, a tempo will feel decidedly too fast or too slow when you listen from a different room, for example. And although the difference between, say, 124 and 125 bpm may be subtle, you may find that one is clearly preferable to the other for a particular context. If you don't get that sense, however, then don't spend more time than necessary worrying about it. Simply choose one and move on.

One interesting phenomenon that's been happening in some recent dubstep and drum and bass is a sense of continuous or fluid shift between half-time and double-time. Because the range of tempos in these genres is relatively fast, music at half speed may sound appropriate when layered with music at the "actual" tempo. A drum and bass track that is predominantly at 170 bpm, for example, might work perfectly well with a sampled breakbeat at 85 bpm. This slow/fast dichotomy allows for a lot of creative flexibility when working in these genres.

And of course, there are no rules when choosing tempo: The correct tempo is the one that makes the song work the best, and this is a creative decision only you can make.

One Part at a Time

"Do not worry. You have always written before and you will write now. All you have to do is write one true sentence. Write the truest sentence that you know."

— Ernest Hemingway, *A Moveable Feast*

Problem:

From the perspective of a blank slate, the idea of "a great song" seems overwhelming and very far away. How can you possibly get from nothing to a complete package—a finished song at the level of the music that inspires you?

You know that songs are made up of lots of parts, and the interplay of those parts is what makes music interesting. But how can you get an interesting interplay of multiple parts when you currently have *nothing at all*?

Solution:

The expression "a journey of a thousand miles begins with a single step" is clichéd but also totally applicable here. Thinking about a finished song from the perspective of a blank project is terrifying, and it's a recipe for paralysis.

So instead, forget about the song for now, and begin writing just one part. Of course, this is obvious: To begin, you have to begin! But treat this one part with the same kind of respect that you would a finished song. Instead of treating it like a building block, a task to accomplish, or a means to an end, try to focus on it as the goal itself. Before you even begin to think about adding more elements, make that one part amazing.

For example, imagine you'll begin with drums (as many producers do). Instead of quickly sketching a pattern with stock sounds and sloppy timing before moving on to a bass line (also quickly sketched), spend the time necessary to completely finish the drums before adding any other elements.

If you've read other music-making tips (including the Breadth Before Depth (page 116) chapter in this book), this may seem counterintuitive. We're commonly told to write by sketching quickly and broadly—many parts, but in little detail—and then treat refinement and editing as something that is done in passes over all of this material. One Part at a Time proposes the opposite approach; instead of working *broadly*, work *deeply* on one element—and only one element—until it's to a level that you would consider release-ready.

This way of working can be valuable for a number of reasons:

> **It helps you to develop the skill of focus.** A single part can be thought of as a tiny version of a complete song. To be successful, both have to satisfy the same basic criteria: They should be sonically (technically) proficient, they should flow well over time, they should

remain interesting upon repeated listening, etc. Meeting these criteria over the course of minutes and with multiple tracks/parts is our ultimate goal, but if we can't make this happen over the course of seconds and with a single part, we're probably doomed. Making yourself finish something small helps you to learn what finishing feels like and helps you to internalize the steps necessary to get there. From there, finishing something larger is just an expanded version of the same process.

> **One great part can reveal more great parts.** Although what's being suggested here is to follow one idea to its end, another positive side effect of this working method is that one idea (especially one great-sounding, inspiring, and completed idea) can lead to others. Hearing a great drum part, with great sounding samples, perfectly placed notes, and attention to every detail, might make you start to imagine complementary bass lines, chords, or melodies.

Of course, it's important to remember not to be too strict in your thinking. (This is true for everything in this book!) If you find that you're getting bored with working on drums and are inspired to work on a bass line instead, follow your inspiration and work on the bass line. But if you're bored with working on one part and *aren't* inspired to work on another one, try applying this technique as an exercise in discipline alone. And if this still isn't working, consider the possibility that the part is unsalvageable—sometimes the best solution is to start over.

Different Tools

Problem:

Your studio tools are like a second home. You've become so comfortable with a particular set of possibilities and workflows that you're able to easily get music made.

But you're not really happy with the results. Your work tends to follow predictable formulas, and you never seem to be able to expand your creative reach. You're pretty sure that your next track will really just be a variation of your last one. And although you're getting songs made, you don't feel like you're really making creative progress.

Gaining a comprehensive understanding of a focused and limited set of tools can be a real creative benefit. Many highly organized electronic musicians are good at resisting gear lust and instead learn a particular DAW inside and out. These same producers are usually equally good at limiting their acquisition of plug-ins and virtual instruments, and instead use either the native devices in their DAW or select plug-ins and/or a small collection of boutique hardware.

This strategy is powerful. It discourages activities like gear experimentation, which feel like music-making but which yield no results. And at the same time, it encourages deep understanding of the tools, which can help eliminate the need to reach for a tutorial in the middle of the creative process.

But these self-imposed limitations can come with a hidden cost—limiting yourself to a concise set of tools may allow you to fall into the mindset of how those tools "think." You may subconsciously begin to make the music suggested by your equipment rather than making the music you really want to make.

Solution:

Even if you're a seasoned veteran with years of experience and carefully thought-out reasons for choosing your studio tools, try making a track using a completely different set of tools. Try changing everything, from your DAW to your plug-ins to your hardware instruments. This is essentially the opposite approach to Mise en Place (page 38)—rather than carefully building a working environment, you're deliberately discarding one you've already built.

The goal here is to break yourself from routines you may not even realize you have. For example, if you've built templates or default presets in your DAW, no matter how much you change them in the course of writing a new track, you're still beginning from the same fixed starting point every time. By completely changing your tools, you're forced to work without these safe havens.

Additionally, you're forced to understand the *mindset* of these new tools. If you enter an unfamiliar creative space, your response to this lack of familiarity might manifest itself as a new creative direction.

For example, if you're a software-only producer, try making a track using hardware synthesizers. Although software instruments can have a strong and unique sonic character, our interaction with them is fundamentally the same from instrument to instrument—we navigate each parameter using the same "controller": a mouse or, at best, a generic hardware controller which is designed to be versatile rather than being focused.

Hardware, on the other hand, offers a physical connection that has a unique physical identity which, in the best cases, is designed in tandem with the sonic identity of the instrument. A synthesizer from one manufacturer uses controls that feel different from those found on a synthesizer from another manufacturer. At some level, this tactile difference must influence the way we approach each instrument.

Furthermore, every tool offers not only its own unique set of possibilities but also its own unique set of limitations and constraints. If you're already comfortable with a particular set of tools, those limitations are well known to you, and you've probably stopped thinking about how they affect your daily work. But by exploring a new environment and following its constraints where they lead you, you'll be forced to make a new set of creative compromises—and, in turn, open a new set of creative possibilities.

Presets as Starting Points

Problem:

You can quickly make music using presets, loop libraries, sample packs, etc. But you're not necessarily comfortable with this approach and are unsure about whether or not it's "cheating."

There is a lot of disagreement and strong opinion about whether or not you can really take credit for your original music if you're not also programming your own sounds. Some electronic musicians are also highly skilled synthesizer programmers and/or sample manipulators, and they talk with pride about how the first thing they do when they get a new piece of equipment is erase all of the presets. Often, the underlying philosophy behind this approach to composition emphasizes *sound* as the principal parameter of the music. Many musicians who focus intensely on sound design also work with a fairly restricted harmonic, melodic, and rhythmic palette. For them, it is timbre choices that largely define their artistic signature. This is common in, for example, minimal techno and some experimental styles.

On the other end of the spectrum are electronic musicians who have no interest in sound design and instead create their music entirely by assembling existing loops and samples. For these musicians, the focus is generally more on harmony, melody, and rhythm, and less on timbre. This is not to suggest that the sounds are arbitrarily chosen or used without care, but rather that there may be a range of acceptable sounds for a particular song part, and that the notes are given more compositional attention than the sounds. This is common in, for example, trance and some house music. In an abstract sense, this is also common in more conventional genres such as classical music or rock. In these genres, the available selection of instruments (and thus the essential palette of sounds) is generally a defining characteristic of the genre, and the composition is then largely about using those instruments in the service of melody, harmony, rhythm, and form.

Which approach is the right one? Perhaps neither. Consider, instead, a middle ground between the two that can maximize musical productivity while minimizing the feeling that you're not taking enough ownership of your music.

Solution:

Instead of approaching sound design as an all-or-nothing endeavor, use presets, samples, and loops as the point of departure for each song part, but with the implicit understanding that you will devote some part of your music-making time to fine-tuning the sounds to suit your particular taste and needs. Purists may always start from a synthesizer's default preset, but this feels like an unnecessary and time-consuming restriction. It means starting from the same state of controls, regardless of intended musical context, and then gradually tuning the sound "outwards" to gain distance from the default. Instead, consider beginning the writing process by using a preset that is at least in the same family as the instrument you're writing for. If you're working on a bass line, for example, explore your synthesizer's bass presets—guilt free. Once you've found one that's as close as possible to the sound you imagine in your head, work on the other parameters of the part: the melody, rhythm, etc. Then, after you have some music underway, come back to the sound again and begin tweaking it so that it takes on your own unique signature.

For musicians with absolutely no sound design experience, this may sound like an intimidating process. But once you learn just the very basics of synthesizer theory, you'll find that this knowledge can be applied to almost any synthesizer. For example, filters and basic ADSR envelope controls can be found on almost any hardware or software synth or sampler. And by using nothing more than these parameters—this is usually no more than six total controls—you can come up with a huge range of variations from a given preset.

Commit at least enough of your music-making time to sound design so that you can be proud of the sounds you use. For the truly discerning electronic musician, it's unlikely that any preset will ever be the perfect choice for their particular musical context. But it might be close. From there, you may need only a few tweaks before you've found something that is uniquely your own.

The Tyranny of the Default

Problem:

Every time you're inspired to start a new song, you open your DAW and are immediately terrified by the blank project. Maybe you have a simple melody, bass line, or drum part in your head. But in order to hear it, you first have to load the appropriate instruments, set the tempo, maybe connect a MIDI controller, etc. By the time you've gotten your DAW to a state where you can actually record, you've either lost the motivation or you've forgotten your original musical idea.

Because DAWs have to cater to a wide range of users, they are often designed to work out of the box with a collection of default options and a basic screen layout that will be offensive to no one but probably also not optimal for anyone. This inevitably leads to a phenomenon that software developers call "the tyranny of the default": Since most users will never change their default software options, the seemingly small decisions made by developers may have a profound effect on the way users will experience the software every day.

Here's how to overcome the tyranny of the default in your own studio.

Solution:

Rather than allowing your DAW to dictate the environment in which you'll start each track, take the time to build your own default or template project. People often think of templates as blank slates containing a bare minimum of elements, and most default templates provided by DAWs are exactly that; maybe one or two empty tracks, perhaps a return track containing a single effect. But if you regularly start work in a similar way (and even if you don't), building a template that's unique to your musical preferences and working style can save you lots of time when you start a new song, allowing you to more quickly capture an initial musical idea from your head into your DAW.

For example, many DAWs set a default tempo of 120 bpm for new projects. If you tend to work in a genre that is generally in a different range of tempos (see Choosing a Tempo (page 50)), save yourself time by saving your template with a more appropriate tempo. Additionally, your DAW's default project likely makes a lot of assumptions about how many output channels you'll be using (usually two), as well as more esoteric settings like sample rate, bit depth, and even the interface's color scheme. If you prefer different settings, don't change them every time you start a new song. Instead, make these changes once and save them in your own template.

Additionally, if you regularly use a particular collection of instruments and/or effects, try pre-loading them into tracks in your DAW and saving them into your template. If you have a go-to sound that you use for sketching out ideas (maybe a sampled piano or a particular preset), preload that preset in your template and even arm the track for recording. This way you can be ready to play and record as soon as the project is loaded.

Some DAWs even allow you to create templates for different types of tracks. For example, if you regularly use a particular combination of effects on each track (such as a compressor and EQ), you could preload these devices—and even customize their parameters—into your default tracks. Then each time you create a new track in any project, you'll have these effects in place without needing to search through your library of devices.

If you regularly work in a variety of genres, you should consider making multiple templates, each one customized for the different sounds and working methods you prefer. Even if your DAW doesn't natively support multiple templates, you can still create your own collection; you'll just need to remember to Save As as soon as you load one, so you don't accidentally overwrite it.

Some producers, recognizing the value of a highly customized template project, have even started selling templates containing nearly (or even completely) finished songs, with the stated goal that newer producers can use these to learn the production techniques of the pros. If that's really how you intend to use them, then these are a potentially valuable learning resource. But be careful to avoid just using these as "construction kits" for your own music. This is potentially worse than working from an empty default and is a gray area between original music and paint-by-numbers copying (or worse, outright plagiarism).

Simple Sounds

Problem:

You have a melodic, harmonic, or rhythmic idea in your head. But when you sit down at your DAW to try to capture it, you usually begin by trying to find or create the right sounds to match the idea. And somewhere along the way, the idea itself gets lost.

As electronic producers, often our first instinct when starting a new song is to collect a palette of sounds before beginning work on the actual notes and rhythms. And modern synthesizer presets are often designed to sound like entire productions just when playing a single note, with huge layers of effects, embedded rhythmic activity, or both.

But sometimes, this can be a distraction from your real goal, which is to create your own compelling musical ideas.

Solution:

Instead of starting by trying to find the perfect sounds, try starting with the simplest sounds you can find. General MIDI or other "generic" presets are good for this exercise.

Now, without taking time to tweak the sounds or add effects, just start working on notes and rhythms. It's likely that everything will sound uninspiring at first, and this is OK. The hope is that by working this way for a while, you'll come across musical ideas that are strong enough to transcend or overcome the sounds that play them. These ideas will have to be *really* good, since they won't be able to hide behind impressive synth patches or layers of effects. But really good ideas are what we're after—musical materials that are so strong that they inspire you on their own merits. Consider that whole symphonies have been written by composers who work entirely at the piano.

Once you have a great collection of self-sufficient musical ideas, then you can start the process of finding great sounds to play them. As you were doing the hard part of the job—writing the music—you may have already had ideas about what kinds of sounds would be appropriate. This will make finding or creating the appropriate sounds even faster and more rewarding, because you'll know that they fit your own musical ideas, rather than suggesting musical ideas that may be more a function of the inherent sonic properties of the sound.

Although generic electronic sounds work well for this, an even better solution is to write using an acoustic instrument like a guitar or piano (if you play one). Acoustic instruments serve dual purposes here. As with General MIDI sounds, they help to get you out of sound-design thinking so you can focus on the music. But they also help you get out of DAW thinking entirely. By removing the computer from the picture for a while, we're more likely to avoid distraction and really force ourselves to write with our ears instead of our eyes.

Of course one challenge of working acoustically is that it makes it a little bit harder to capture great moments of inspiration that would otherwise automatically land in your DAW. In this case, it might help to set up a mic in the room and record everything you play as audio. Yes, it might take a bit more work to then sort out what you played later, but at least the ideas won't be lost.

This technique isn't for every producer. If your music is fundamentally *about* sound design, then it's possible that notes and rhythms aren't much of a factor in your work at all. In such cases, these techniques will probably just waste time. But if you're a producer working in a less experimental genre, starting with simple sounds might help you get to better music.

Extended Techniques

Problem:

You're generally bored with the sounds that you've been using. Your real-world samples all sound too real, and your electronic sounds all sound too conventionally electronic. You're looking for something that bridges the gap between the rawness of acoustic sounds and the flexibility of synthesis. You've tried using effects to process your sounds but this just feels like adding a fresh coat of paint. You need something really new.

Sampling from the acoustic world brings a layer of "realness" to electronic music productions that is difficult to achieve using synthesis alone. And although samplers and effects can help to turn real-world sources into something radically different, here are some lo-tech ways to get entirely new sounds from acoustic sources.

Solution:

Although it's always possible to use samplers and effects to modify source sounds into something completely different, it can also be inspiring to work with a sound that's already unusual on its own. Field recordings, found sounds, and other types of non-instrumental source material have long been used as fodder for samplers, but there is also a world of new sound possibilities available from instruments you already know.

The term "extended techniques" refers to unconventional approaches to sound production using conventional instruments. Probably the most familiar extended technique is the "prepared piano" made famous by John Cage (among others). Cage's scores for prepared piano call for objects such as bolts and rubber erasers to be placed on or between the piano strings, or on the hammers or dampers. The resultant sound varies widely depending on the particular type of preparation used, but often sounds like a diverse collection of metallic percussion instruments.

Another extended technique that can yield great results is the use of stringed instrument bows on other objects. A lot of contemporary percussion music, for example, calls for bowed vibraphone bars, cymbals, gongs, and other metal objects. In fact, almost any piece of resonant metal can be activated via bowing. If you have access to a bow, try bowing pots and pans, metal furniture, etc. And if you don't have access to a real bow, you can create makeshift bows out of fishing line.

There are a variety of possible extended techniques for woodwind and brass instruments. If you have access to these instruments (as well as adventurous people who can play them), try playing them without their reeds or mouthpieces, playing only the reed or mouthpiece, or even using the mouthpiece from one instrument on another "wrong" instrument. In some cases, this will produce no sound at all, but you can sometimes get very interesting timbres by resonating these instruments in new ways.

Woodwind and brass instruments are also capable of producing multiple simultaneous pitches, which are known as *multiphonics*. For woodwinds, multiphonics are produced by using certain unconventional fingerings, while on brass instruments they can be produced by humming additional pitches while playing normally.

In recent years, the concept of extended techniques has moved beyond the world of acoustic instruments and into the electronic domain as well. The practice known as *circuit bending* is the physical modification of electronic sound-making devices with the goal of creating sounds those devices were never intended to make. Common circuit bending targets are cheap electronic instruments, children's toys, etc. Circuit bent instruments can be a great source of new timbres, particularly because they often produce very unusual sounds while still retaining the lo-fi character of the original device.

Goal-less Exploration

Problem:

You're sitting in front of your DAW, but you're uninspired. You've opened the DAW out of habit, or because you know you should, or because you have the abstract feeling of wanting to make music, but you have no real sense that you actually want to make anything in particular. This feels frustrating, and like wasted time. Maybe you should just close the DAW and try again another day.

Many of us are happy once a song is finished, but often we find the process of actually making the song to be painful, boring, or unrewarding. Sometimes we might reach a point where we see that the end of the song is in sight, and then we're inspired by the prospect of having something to show for our work. But until that point, it really does feel like work. How can you generate inspiration? Just opening a new project sometimes isn't enough.

Solution:

If you've already taken the step to open your DAW, you should congratulate yourself; this is farther than many musicians got today. Our computers (and even the real world) offer endless distractions that can prevent us from even beginning work. And although our underlying goal is to get music made, sometimes this is too much of a responsibility to bear. Even though you don't feel like working, once the DAW is open, there are a number of things you can do to seize the moment, even if it's a brief one.

Goal-less exploration is the process of simply finding a corner of your working space and letting yourself see what evolves from there. For example, maybe there's a particular instrument or effect in your DAW that you've never taken the time to learn or that you've tried to use but never could find a place for in your music. Since the DAW is open anyway, try loading these devices and just experimenting with them. Without the pressure of trying to use them to make music, just spend some time learning what sorts of sounds they can make.

Another type of goal-less exploration can come from taking some time and going through your loop and sample library. If you're like most producers, you've probably collected far more samples than you've ever had time to really listen to. If you don't feel like working on music, explore those folders of samples and see what you actually have.

Working in this kind of free, non-directed way can sometimes unlock creative directions that you never would have found in your normal working process, when you might be tempted to use templates or known tools in order to get going more quickly. If goal-less exploration actually manages to turn into real, finished work, then all the better. But you're also not under any obligation to turn your explorations into a finished song, or even the beginning of one. Maybe you'll work for a long time and find that you've created nothing worth saving. This is OK. The point here is that you're doing something that is at least in the realm of music-making; this is already closer to where you want to be than, for example, Facebook.

There are so many things you can do in a DAW that aren't directly focused on the creation and completion of a song. If your DAW is open, but your normal creative inspiration isn't there, try simply exploring and see where it leads.

Procrastination and Timeboxing

Problem:

In the abstract, you know that you want to make music. But the actual process of doing it sometimes feels like torture.

You know that working on music can bring moments of bliss: When the work is going well, the music sounds great, and you're in a state of flow. But there seem to be as many or more moments of agony. Despite our best intentions, there are lots of reasons why we sometimes procrastinate, including fear of failure, fear of success, and simple laziness.

In the chapter called On Work (page 112), we discuss the inevitable reality that working is the only way to actually make progress. But here is a tip for actually getting to work.

Solution:

If you're a chronic procrastinator, you're not alone. Many creative (and non-creative) people suffer from task aversion and can find any excuse to avoid getting done the work that really needs to get done. One strategy for overcoming procrastination that's commonly used in the software development world is known as *timeboxing*.

Timeboxing simply means setting a fixed amount of time for a particular task. The amount of time you choose is up to you, but it should be short enough so that it's easily manageable by even the most determined procrastinators. For example, you might decide to spend 20 minutes on sound design. Next, set a timer, work only on sound design, and stop when the timer goes off. Finally, take a short break (five minutes or so). Then repeat the process, perhaps with another unrelated type of task (e.g., drum programming, arranging, etc.). After four or five stretches of this timed work/break combo, you might want to take a longer break.

Short timeboxes work because they break apart intimidating, open-ended tasks into easily manageable chunks; no matter how painful creative work is, anyone can do it for 20 minutes. It's important that you really work during those 20 minutes—intensely and without interruption. But it's equally important that you stop at the end. No matter how productive you are or how close you feel to entering a real flow state, stick to the timebox. This may seem counterintuitive; after all, if you've finally managed to trick yourself into enjoying the process, doesn't it make sense to run with that as far as your attention span will allow? But the reason this is dangerous (at least at first) is because it runs the risk of setting you up for a long work session that eventually becomes frustrating or disappointing. When this happens, your memory of the session will be that it was both bad and long-lasting, which may further reinforce your procrastination tendencies. On the other hand, if you stop even while it's fun, you're more likely to be energized and ready to move forward again once the break is over.

After you spend a few days sticking to a systematic timeboxing routine, you may find that your latent procrastination starts to feel less overbearing, and you feel the urge to just do uninterrupted work. At this point, you might first try using longer and longer timeboxes. Eventually, you may find yourself able to focus without assistance at all and can then consider your procrastination cured. And if you find yourself slipping back to your old work-avoidance habits later, simply try using the timer again.

Collaboration

Problem:

You're considering the possibility of working with other musicians but aren't sure how to proceed. What do you look for in a collaborator? What should their role be in the creative process?

Musical collaboration can be a hugely rewarding catalyst for creativity, in which the resulting music is more than the sum of the individuals who made it. But establishing the *right* collaboration is critical; working with the wrong partner can be more painful than working alone. Here are some tips for finding great musical partners.

Solution:

When deciding on a partner for musical collaboration, the most important consideration is simply whether or not the partnership will result in better and/or more music. It's tempting to imagine that your best friend will also be your ideal musical partner, but personal compatibility and professional compatibility aren't necessarily related. Sure, the process will likely be more fun if you're working with someone with whom you have a good social connection. But many personal relationships have been destroyed by attempting to extend them into professional relationships; if the professional one fails, the personal one might as well. If your best friend happens to also have a strong work ethic and great musical and technical skills, then the partnership might make sense. But if not, consider partnering with someone else. Of course, even the most talented musician isn't going to work out in the long run if they're a horrible person. But when in doubt, aim for professional compatibility first and social compatibility second.

Whenever possible, try to work with people who can counterbalance your strengths and weaknesses. The most obvious example is the classic "producer plus vocalist" partnership. The producer deals with all of the musical and technical aspects of the song, while the vocalist brings a particular talent that the producer simply doesn't have. Beyond this obvious example, try to find partners who are good at a particular aspect of the production process that you're bad at or that you dislike. For example, if you have trouble with arrangements, try to find a partner who excels at them. If you're good at sound design and synth programming, don't worry too much about finding a partner who also has these skills (although two completely well-rounded collaborators might be the ideal package).

Although the traditional model of collaboration involves multiple musicians in the same studio, recent technological advancements also make it possible to collaborate with people remotely, and possibly even anonymously. For example, the classic model of the studio musician has changed in recent years, and many session musicians who used to show up for recording studio dates are now tracking parts for a variety of projects from their home studios, sometimes without ever meeting the artists for whom they're recording. This type of workflow is even easier for electronic musicians, because there's no need for acoustic treatment, microphone setups, etc. For example, perhaps you have an idea for a synth part that's beyond your ability to play. Using remote collaboration tools, you might find someone to record the part you need and deliver it back to you, entirely online.

Once you've found a good collaborative situation, it's important that everyone involved understands exactly how things like workload, money, ownership, and creative rights are to be divided. Misunderstandings can result in a lot of misery for all parties, so it's best to have clear conversations and real, mutual understanding as early as possible.

Thinking Like an Amateur

Problem:

Ever since you started getting "serious" about your music-making, you've secretly started having less fun with it. You (vaguely) remember a time when you didn't feel this way; when you had no aspirations to be a professional, making music was always a great way for you to relax. But now that you've become concerned with "success," your sense of childlike joy at just making sounds has disappeared and has been overtaken by your desire to *finish songs*—or even scarier: *get famous*.

Although this book is mostly about finding ways to get music done, sometimes there are benefits to forgetting about that way of thinking entirely and instead just enjoying the process of making music as a goal in itself.

Solution:

When someone is referred to as an amateur, this is usually meant to imply that they're less qualified or less talented than a professional in the same field. An amateur, it's assumed, is someone who would have liked to be a professional but who was unable to reach that level. But despite these negative connotations, the word "amateur" actually just means "lover of," and there are many amateurs in all fields who are working at a very high level. And there are still many more who aren't necessarily great at what they do but are having a great time.

Think about something you consider a hobby, something (besides music) that you do with your free time. Maybe you run marathons, or brew beer, or take wildlife photographs. Whatever it is, have you ever even considered doing it professionally? Probably not. And most likely this isn't because you're not good enough (and whether you are or not is probably irrelevant to your decision), but rather because the very fact that it's a hobby means that it's something you do that *isn't work*. Instead, it's a chance to spend time on something fun and fulfilling that doesn't saddle you with any outside pressure to succeed, earn a living, etc.

Electronic musicians, more so than musicians working in other genres, seem to have a more difficult time simply engaging with music as a hobby. Perhaps this is because tools like DAWs are fundamentally designed around a recording mentality. Think about people you've met who own an acoustic guitar. Just pulling it out and playing it for a few minutes while sitting on the couch may be the extent of their musical aspirations. And they don't see this as failure. They're not lamenting their inability to get gigs or write more music or get record deals. They're having exactly the relationship with music that they want. In fact, they're usually not even recording what they play; once it's in the air, it's gone.

By definition, being a professional means having to spend at least some amount of time thinking about the marketplace. Is there an audience for the music you're making? If not, you're guaranteed to fail. Amateurs, on the other hand, never have to think about this question at all. This frees them to make music entirely for themselves, on their own terms.

One easy way to do this is to put yourself into a musical context in which you actually *are* an amateur—by experimenting with a genre in which you have no prior experience. Are you a committed hip-hop producer? Try making a house track. Your expectations are bound to be lower, simply because you have no prior successes or failures against which to gauge your current work. Even if you hate the results, it's likely that you'll learn something from the experience.

Even if you do aspire to make a living out of creating original music, it might be helpful to think like an amateur in order to lower your stress and bring the fun back to your music-making time. Amateurs often have a genuinely more pleasurable experience than professionals working in the same field, and this is almost certainly because they're free from outside pressure. If you can instill this mindset into your own work, you'll probably have both better results and a better time.

Scraps and Sketches

Problem:

Your hard drive is filled with unfinished songs, and you know that most of them aren't worth finishing. Whenever you look at these songs, you're frustrated because you feel like you've failed and that you have nothing to show for all of the work and time you've spent on them.

We abandon music for a lot of reasons. Sometimes we realize that we're not happy with the direction the song is taking. Sometimes we just get bored, go do something else, and then never come back to the work in progress. While I'm a strong advocate of finishing bad songs anyway (see Fail Better (page 340)), the reality is that most producers either have folders full of abandoned projects that will never be opened again, or they throw away work in progress if it stops being interesting. Here's an idea for making use of that unfinished material.

Solution:

Rather than considering your folder of unfinished projects as trash or wasted effort, consider it as a collection of scraps or sketches, ready for reuse in other musical contexts. This way, you can start a new song by extracting elements of abandoned or unfinished songs from the past, rather than facing the intimidating blank slate of a completely empty project. Forget entirely that these were once supposed to be "songs," and instead treat them as collections of musical ideas that are ready to be used again: your own custom—and completely unique—sound and loop library.

You may already be keeping a folder of scraps and sketches, either as a result of Goal-less Exploration (page 78) or perhaps by collecting rejected audio files created by Rendering as Commitment (page 330). The only difference here is that you're rehabilitating and recycling material that you once intended to be used in an actual, active composition. This can be incredibly liberating mentally, because it allows you to reject the idea that an unfinished song is a failure and instead embrace it as a collection of ammunition for the next song.

So throw away as little as you can. Even if you're bored after a single two-bar drum loop or bass line, save this work into your sketches folder. It's possible that it will become the basis of your next great song.

Problem-Solving as Distraction

Problem:

Every time you go to make music, you realize that there's something wrong with your setup; a plug-in you need isn't authorized, or you forgot to download a sample pack that you purchased, or your chair isn't comfortable. You dream of the day when you can hire a studio assistant to take care of all of the busy work that seems to be in your way every time you want to make music. But until then, you're not sure how to get anything done when all of these problems keep coming up. How do other people do it?

Technical problems in the studio can really kill the creative flow. Similarly, realizing that you don't fully understand a particular production process or how to use a particular piece of gear can be frustrating—particularly when you had planned to use those things in the course of your current song. When faced with these situations, here's how to get work done anyway.

Solution:

Ignore these problems. They're not as important as you think.

Steven Pressfield, in his classic book *The War of Art*, talks about a force that manifests in the life of creative people in order to keep them from getting work done. He calls this force Resistance. These problems you're finding in your studio are a manifestation of Resistance. It's a trap! Your mind is playing tricks on you to try to keep you from working. None of these problems are serious enough to take time away from your creative efforts. If they were, you would have solved them already, during your non-productive time. The only reason you notice them when you sit down to work is that part of you doesn't want to sit down to work.

Technical problem solving, education, motivational reading (including this book), and other forms of work-related activities will never write music for you. They're important, but as discussed in On Work (page 112), they're nowhere near as important as actually *doing the work*.

Your creative time is essential; you should treat it with care and recognize when you're subconsciously trying to avoid it. If you suddenly realize that a plug-in you need isn't authorized, then use another one. You don't need it right now. You've made music without it before, and you can make music without it now. If you forgot to download a sample pack you purchased, use some samples you already have. If your chair isn't comfortable, work anyway. You can fix your chair on your next break or when the song's done (whichever comes first).

Nothing seems to stimulate the need to learn production techniques like sitting down to work. Do you really need to learn more about EQ or compression right now? Watch tutorial videos later; now is the time to work.

This is not to suggest that learning and problem solving aren't important. It's just that they belong to a different type of working time. The chapter Mise en Place (page 38) discusses the importance of setting up your environment to be maximally conducive to getting work done. But as important as this is, it's even more important that it be done at the right time. And the right time is *never* when you're in the creative mindset.

Music-making time is sacred. Don't stop to learn and don't stop to fix something unless it's absolutely critical. Use what you have and know, right now, to keep going forward.

Personal Workflow

Problem:

The more you read about music production techniques, the more you get the sense that you're doing everything wrong. For example, some tutorials advocate working on sound design, composition, arranging, and mixing in that order and as entirely separate processes. Others recommend doing them all at the same time and working each section of the song to completion in all aspects before moving to a different part of the song. But none of these solutions feels quite right, and now you're more confused and discouraged than you were before you read anything. What is *really* the optimum workflow?

Reading multiple tutorials or books about music production can make you feel suspicious that it's all just subjective. There seems to be so much disagreement from one source to the next that it all feels somewhat arbitrary. Who has the right answers?

Solution:

When it comes to optimal workflow, there is no objective right answer. The only way you can find a workflow that's optimal for you is by trying out various methods, keeping the parts that work, rejecting the parts that don't, and synthesizing your own solution out of what remains. When you're reading a tutorial, you're really reading about a workflow that has worked for that particular writer. A different writer may have had an entirely different experience, and so will have advocated an entirely different approach.

If you have trouble getting music done, it's worth looking at the workflows that other people advocate and giving them a try. But don't expect that any one person's approach will yield better results for your particular case than an approach that you develop yourself. It's true that when trying out another method you may see a dramatic shift in your productivity (either positively or negatively). If things are better, then it's likely you've found a direction that's better than the one you were on before. If things are worse, you should probably abandon this direction and try something else. But in the end, even the best third-party workflow will benefit from your own personal tweaks and modifications.

Once you have the sense that you're going in the right direction, the key to optimizing your personal workflow is to practice it until it becomes a habit. Practice the steps just as you would practice an instrument, refining and adjusting as you go. Eventually, the workflow will stop being work and just become flow—the things you do unconsciously while creating.

This all sounds quite abstract, but there really aren't so many possible things to consider. At a fundamental level, music production workflows all involve answers to the following questions:

> What are the things I need to do?
> Is there an order I should do them in? If so, what is it?

> When should I move on to the next thing?
> When do I know I'm completely done?

Once you understand how to answer these questions—for yourself, not as absolutes—you will have developed your personal workflow. All that's left to do is make music with it.

Originality vs. Quality

Problem:

You're happy with the music you make, and other people are as well. But deep down, you don't believe it's truly original, and you feel that you should be working harder to find a sound that is uniquely your own.

Particularly among music critics, journalists, and bloggers, originality is regularly cited as a necessary component of good music. Pejorative terms like "derivative" or "formulaic" are often used to deride music that sounds like something else. But what critics write is not always what listeners hear, and there may be different ways of weighing musical value.

Solution:

What does originality actually mean in a musical context? As a descriptor, all it tells you is that something sounds unique, or that its influences are not obvious. But what the word doesn't convey is any information about quality, which is a far more valuable characteristic. "Original" and "good" are not mutually exclusive, but they are also not correlated. There is plenty of terrible music that sounds like nothing else, and in many cases the very characteristics that make it original are also what make it bad. Consider that what one artist thinks is original may simply be something that other artists have already tried and discarded.

Instead of aiming for an abstract goal like originality, aim instead for the concrete goal of *quality*. This is not to suggest that you should actively try to make your music sound like something else, but rather that you should try to find and strengthen your own voice through a process of constant, varied listening, experimentation, synthesis of disparate influences, and—above all—hard work. If you only listen to a small variety of music, there are really only two conceivable outcomes for your own creations: Either you'll make things that reflect your limited exposure or you'll make things that you believe are original but are more than likely simply outside of your experience.

Even if you really only want to make music within a particular, narrow genre, you should *still* aim for a wide range of listening experiences. For example, imagine you only want to make old-school house tracks. Since a characteristic of that style is sampled phrases from jazz, soul, and R&B records, wouldn't an understanding of those genres be a valuable tool in your creative arsenal? Wouldn't understanding how jazz drummers and bass players approach rhythm and harmony help your own rhythm and harmony? And if you end up making old-school house music that fits perfectly into the confines of the genre, no one can claim that you're original. But if the music is good, that's all that matters.

In the end, the music that's remembered is not necessarily the music that's the most radically avant-garde. Instead, it's the music that's good. If you can achieve both quality and originality, then you're a rarity. But the primary goal should always be quality first.

Process vs. Product

Problem:

Often we read interviews with interesting musicians in which they talk about the monumental effort that goes into their creative work. Similarly, they may talk about how their music is rigorously structured or adheres to particular types of architectural processes that are carefully and painstakingly planned and then require immense work to carry out. When we then go to work on our own music, it may feel like we're "under thinking" or not investing enough effort. We may begin work but then stop and second-guess what we've made if we don't feel like we've done enough preparation to allow us to really begin "properly."

The idea of "process" in music refers to the development of a system or set of rules that allows some or all of the elements of the music to be generated or derived without requiring the composer to make purely intuitive creative decisions at every possible moment. There is a belief in our culture, often reinforced by interviews with celebrities, that there is a necessary and direct correlation between process and quality. For musicians who work intuitively, or via improvisation and experiment, this narrative can be intimidating. How can it be possible to create great work if we don't have a grand scheme and/or long hours of struggle?

Solution:

First, take every interview with a grain of salt. Interviews allow artists to share insights into their working methods, but interviews can also serve a valuable self-promotional function. There is nothing wrong with this—artists should take advantage of opportunities to present themselves. But readers should not expect an interview to reveal absolute truths, and stories about struggles, hard work, and rigorous planning might simply serve to help an artist create and publicly project a romantic or idealized self-image.

Second, effort, rigor, pre-planning, and structure are not prerequisites for quality results. They may help you get there, but they are neither necessary to begin work nor, in themselves, evidence for quality. It's tempting to believe that things we've spent a lot of time and energy on are worth it, but in the case of music, only the results matter. Some listeners may indeed actively listen for musical structure, and the intricacy, depth, or cohesiveness of that structure may be what determines for them whether or not the music is "good." Likewise, some listeners may enjoy music because it sounds "difficult." Consider, for example, certain types of virtuosic metal or progressive rock, in which technical ability is a prerequisite. But there is no universal relationship between artistic effort and artistic quality. Many listeners take in music on a much more immediate and visceral level and enjoy particular music for reasons which may be more difficult to quantify.

Think of the process of creation as something like the scaffolding on a building. It's placed there to help the builders navigate the unsteadiness of a fragile work in progress. But once the building is completed, the scaffolding is removed and promptly forgotten. It is not, in itself, the thing being made. It may have curiosity value to other builders, who may have an abstract interest in the artifacts of construction. But good scaffolding cannot guarantee a good building any more than a good working process can guarantee a good song.

Furthermore, there is the danger that too much time invested in planning how you'll work will both prevent you from actually working *and* cause you to accept results that sound bad just because they fit the plan. For example, imagine you've spent hours crafting a four-minute song in which the second two minutes are a literal mirror image of the first two. This is an interesting idea in the abstract. It provides a path forward: Once you've finished two minutes of music, you now have a system for how to finish two more through the simple application of a formula. But is it a good idea? Only the results can determine this. At the end, the product—not the process—is what you're left with, and the product needs to be strong enough to survive on its own.

This is not to suggest that you shouldn't experiment with employing processes in your music. Maybe a song with a mirrored form really will end up being amazing. And even if it isn't, you may end up learning something about how mirroring works as a musical process that can be applied in different ways in future works. What's important is that you don't fall so in love with the idea of what your music should be (or the work that you've put into it) that you fail to honestly judge it on the basis of how it really sounds when you've finished. Better yet: Listen critically at every stage of the process, and be willing to abandon conceptual directions if they are leading to bad musical results.

There is a rich history of brilliant music made by musicians who started without a grand scheme and simply followed where their experiments or improvisations led them. Furthermore, there is an equally rich tradition of brilliant music that was made very quickly and with seemingly little effort. Again, the important thing is the song—the final result of the work. What's unimportant (or, more accurately, what's not a reliable predictor of quality) is everything leading up to that point: the sketches and careful planning diagrams, the months spent in the studio, etc.

If those things really are the way that you get to a great result, then you should absolutely do them. But do not convince yourself that those things will guarantee a great result.

On Work

"Genius is one percent inspiration and ninety-nine percent perspiration."
— Thomas Edison

"Inspiration is for amateurs—the rest of us just show up and get to work."
— Chuck Close

Problem:

Sometimes, there are moments during the creative process when you get into a state of flow, music seems to come out naturally, and everything feels effortless. But this is extremely rare. Most of the time, working on music feels like a thankless chore.

How is it that some musicians seem to be able to produce endless amounts of music in minimal time, while you feel like every note is a struggle? What's the secret to finding the mythical "flow" state that will enable you to create music effortlessly?

Solution:

The reality is that there are no shortcuts. The process of creating art is, fundamentally, a process of *work*. For most of us, every note really is a struggle, and this is simply the nature of the process. We have a romantic image of the artistic genius, who is able to spin endless amounts of material out of nothing, but these types of artists are extremely rare.

Rather than aspiring to this mysterious (and unrealistic) notion of what the process should be, try instead to embrace what it really is: hard work. There will be many points along the creative path when you'll wish you were doing almost anything else. You will be plagued with doubt, fear, boredom, and disappointment. Learn to be OK with being miserable, because this will be a regular part of your existence as a creative musician.

By all means, if you do happen to find moments of inspiration and real flow, you should embrace them and let them take you as far as they can. But even in these rare cases, it's usually only after a lot of painful effort that effortlessness takes over. Even the most fortunate, flow-prone artists don't just get there immediately. As painful as it is, every project, for everyone, requires real work.

Problems of Progressing

Breadth Before Depth

Problem:

Whenever you start making progress on a track, you suddenly become overwhelmed by the desire to get some particular aspect completely perfect. For example, maybe you're preoccupied with getting the sound of your kick drum just right. Lots of time can be spent in this phase, and it often becomes frustrating, sapping your will to continue working on the track as a whole.

Since you know that you'll eventually have to refine every aspect anyway, can there be a downside to doing at least some of that refinement as you go?

Solution:

Especially in the early and middle stages of your work on a track, when the ideas themselves may not exist yet, it can be detrimental to go into too much depth in any one particular area. Yes, you'll need to do detail work eventually. But the idea-generation phase is vital and very, very fragile. By definition, it's messy and doesn't hold up well when confronted with outside pressures. Idea generation requires experimentation, risk-taking, unbounded thinking, etc. Detail work, on the other hand, is an entirely different kind of working process and requires an entirely different mindset. Detail work requires narrow, focused thinking. It's often more about applying known processes than it is about exploring radical new directions.

When you're in idea-generation mode, it can be useful to work broadly—getting ideas out of your head and into the sequencer as quickly as possible—before working deeply on a single part. This way of working can be valuable for a number of reasons:

> **It helps you to learn how to listen for potential rather than for perfection.** During broad idea generation, parts might sound bad for a variety of reasons. Maybe you have a terrible mix balance, or the wrong sounds, or even some wrong notes. But you've drawn inspiration from music that has none of these problems—finished, mastered tracks have a professional sheen that's miles ahead of where your particular track is right now. This can be discouraging, because even though we know that we can add polish at the end, we want to hear it *right now*. If your music doesn't compare to your inspiration at this moment, how can you be sure that you're going in the right direction? The key here is to practice learning to listen past the imperfections: Instead of thinking "this bass line isn't powerful enough," think "this bass line *can* be powerful enough after some sound design work and mixing. But how are the notes?" By hearing past the immediate lack of impact, you become a better judge of whether or not a particular part (or the whole track) is going in the right direction.

- **Creative time is short, and you have to move fast.** As mentioned previously, the idea-generation phase is fragile. It's the one part of the music creation process that you can't "force" to happen. This means that when it actually is happening, you need to squeeze out every idea that you can, working as quickly as possible and generating as much material as possible before your mind moves out of this phase. Once you've captured the ideas, the work of actually refining them can sometimes require much less truly creative energy.

This suggestion runs directly counter to the chapter called One Part at a Time (page 54). The reality is that there is no one way to work; different types of creative blocks may be solved in fundamentally different, and even opposing, ways.

Foreground, Middle Ground, and Background

Problem:

Your music has a feeling of "flatness" or two-dimensionality that is somewhat difficult to explain. The music that inspires you definitely doesn't suffer from this, although you find it equally difficult to express what it is, specifically, that's more satisfying about those inspiring songs.

Typically, we think of different instruments and/or voices in a song as having different levels of prominence. And we probably have some instinctive ideas about how to reinforce these levels of prominence when working on a mix. For example, important sounds are typically mixed louder than less important ones.

But creating a sense of varied "depth" in music is more complicated than just applying basic mixing rules. By thinking about depth even during the composition phase, we can complement our mixing decisions and create an even stronger sense that each element is fulfilling a specific functional role.

Solution:

The notion of foreground, middle ground, and background are well known to anyone who works in the visual arts: film, photography, painting, etc. In visual art, these layers refer to objects at different physical distances from the viewer's eye.

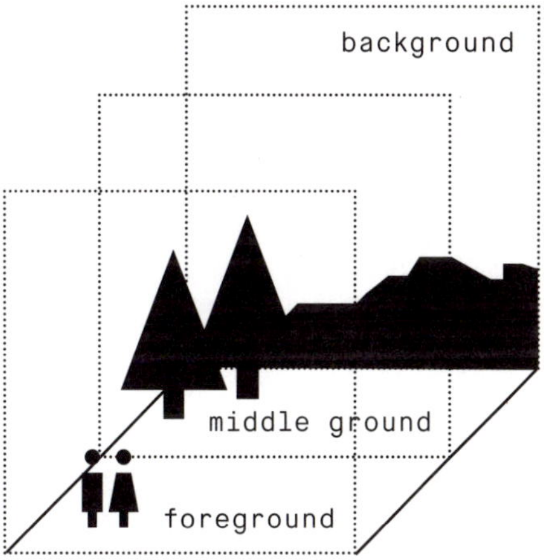

Typically, the objects in the foreground are the ones with the most prominence. In a photograph, for example, foreground objects are commonly the "subject" of the composition. They're often in focus, and we can see the complexity and fine detail. The background, on the other hand, contains objects in the far distance. We recognize them, but they might be blurry or otherwise less rich in detail. The middle ground contains everything else—objects which are generally not the primary focus of our attention but which are closer (and thus more prominent) than those in the background.

At a technical or production level, this concept can also be applied to an audio recording, and this is what mix engineers refer to when they talk about the "depth" of a mix. For example, sounds can be made to seem closer to the listener by making them louder, "brighter" (an increase in high-frequency content in comparison to other sounds), and/or "dryer" (an increase in the amount of original, unprocessed signal in comparison to the amount of reverb applied to that signal). Likewise, sounds can be placed in the background by making them quieter, darker, or more reverberant.

But even before the mixing stage, we can think of our musical elements themselves as being divided into foreground, middle ground, and background. For example, in a track with a singer, we usually want the voice to be the most important element. We can try to force this to happen when mixing, but we can also make musical decisions to enhance the effect. For example, imagine a scenario in which the vocal melody is doubled note for note by a synth line that plays an octave higher. Our ears are naturally drawn to the highest sound in a mix, so we might subconsciously hear the synth line as the dominant voice. In an even more extreme example, imagine that our accompanying synth didn't double the voice but instead played a line that was more complicated, with faster rhythms, jagged jumps from note to note, etc. We would probably hear this as still more prominent.

We tend to hear things as being in the foreground if they're *high*, *loud*, *fast*, or *subject to a rapid rate of change*. For example, the drum groove of a song is often quite loud in comparison to the rest of the mix. But because it's also generally consistent and unvarying in relation to the other voices, we're able to place it in its appropriate place in the texture: the middle ground or background. When a drum fill happens, however, the sudden change in textural density and complexity causes us to switch our focus to the drums; they temporarily jump to the foreground.

When writing music, try to think about where each element should reside on this three-layered depth chart of foreground, middle ground, and background. Draw the elements in a box like the one in the previous picture if it helps you to visualize. Or simpler yet, just make a list. Here's an example of what a list of song parts for a minimal techno track might look like if divided into foreground/middle ground/ background:

Foreground

> Pitch-shifted spoken text (irregular, mostly non-rhythmic)
> Metal clang "interruptions" (irregular, high-pitched, loud)

Middle ground

> Synth bleeps (medium pitch, repeating patterns)
> Synth marimba chords (medium pitch, repeating patterns)
> Acid bass line (medium pitch, repeating patterns; sometimes comes to foreground via brighter filter settings, variations in the pattern)

Background

> Drums (steady-state)
> Sub bass (steady-state, low pitch)

Each element in the list is followed by decisions about musical parameters which will help to reinforce the selected depth. The rate of change in the middle ground and background elements is kept to a minimum, while foreground elements are allowed more freedom of motion.

Additionally, try to experiment with making temporary changes in the depth at which certain voices reside, as in the drum fill example mentioned before. By varying the depth of elements in a song, we also draw attention to the fact that we're using depth in the first place, which helps to reinforce the overall effect.

Fuzzy Boundaries

Problem:

DAWs tend to automatically structure material in blocks (often called "clips" or "regions") with clearly defined beginnings and endings. Musical structure is then created by moving the blocks around in time, but the sharp edges between the blocks also create a specific type of musical abruptness which may sound stiff, formulaic, and unrefined.

Most pieces of music divide time into sections, where each section contains a particular type of musical material that contrasts with that in the other sections. Additionally, these sections often exist within a hierarchy of sectional layers, with smaller contrasting subsections chained together to form the larger sections. In the abstract, this hierarchy might look something like this:

`clip —• phrase —• song section —• whole song`

DAWs represent this musical structure in a very clear way; blocks of time appear as literal blocks on the screen. But the boundaries of these blocks suggest boundaries in time that are not always good representations of the musical results we want. Here are some ways to make the boundaries between formal sections less abrupt.

Solutions:

Abrupt formal boundaries look like a straight vertical line that cuts through the material in your tracks from top to bottom:

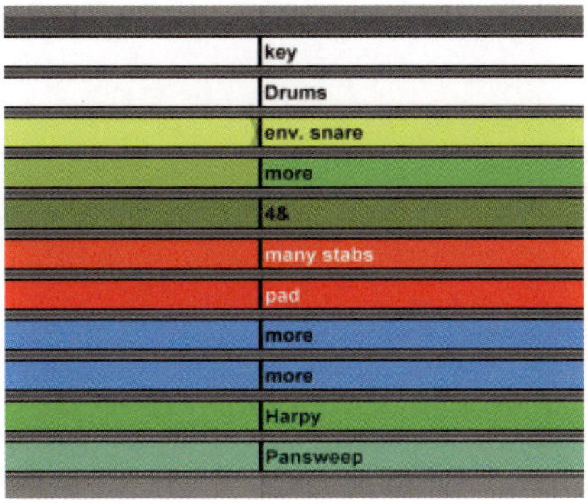

The most straightforward way to deal with this kind of abruptness is to simply make that line become jagged or disappear entirely by:

> extending material from the previous section in one or more (but not all) tracks.
> retracting material from the previous section in one or more (but not all) tracks.
> deleting material on either side of the formal boundary in one or more tracks.

For example, here's how this formal division might look after applying all of these techniques:

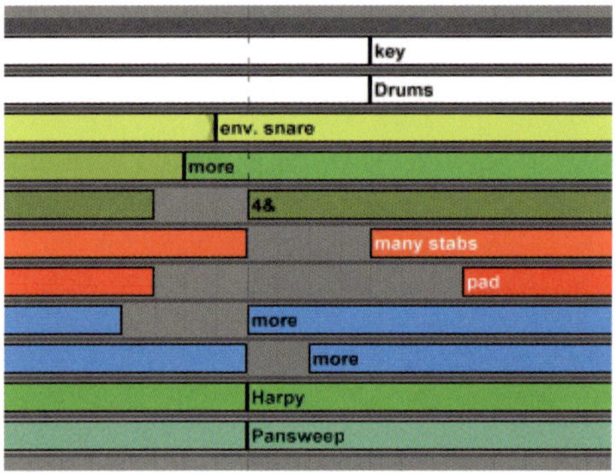

In this example, only the bottom two tracks have been left as they were in the original version. The top two tracks have had material extended beyond the formal boundary, while the next two tracks transition early. The following five tracks all use silence to blur the transition.

~ Note that this example is not a prescription for a particular set of actions; there's nothing inherent about this particular pattern of changes that will make sense in all cases. Of course, it's necessary to adapt what you do to the specifics of the material in your song.

These kinds of "coarse-grained" changes to the length and position of clips can be effective. But sometimes you'll want to edit the material within the clips themselves. Here are some "fine-grained" ways to think about working with this material:

Anticipation - Drum fills are a common technique used to create a sense of transition from one section to another. But it's common to hear drum fills that lead out of one section and then end precisely on the downbeat of the next section. Here's an example of a "typical" drum fill that ends exactly on a downbeat. The energy peaks at the downbeat of bar 3:

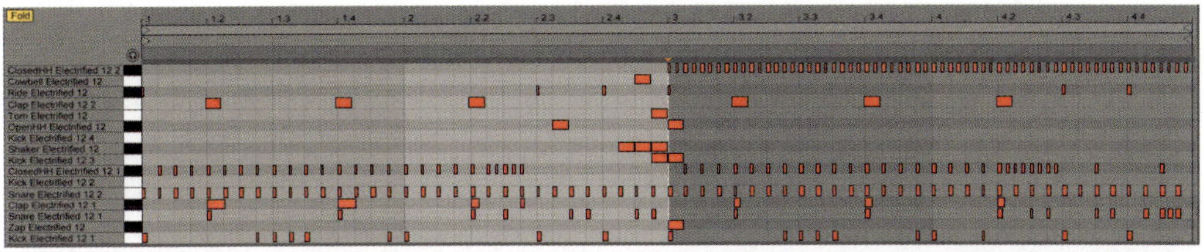

This is often musically effective, but it can sometimes feel formulaic and abrupt. Instead, try writing drum fills that *anticipate*, or end slightly earlier than expected. Reaching the peak of a fill slightly before the downbeat, for example, can create an interesting shift in the flow of musical time. This can be particularly effective if the actual downbeat is de-emphasized somehow, perhaps by stopping the drums entirely until the second beat of the next section, and then re-entering with a "crash" or some other moment that emphasizes the sense of a musical ending. Here's an example of a drum fill that anticipates the sectional boundary. The energy peaks before the downbeat, followed by silence and a re-entrance on beat 2:

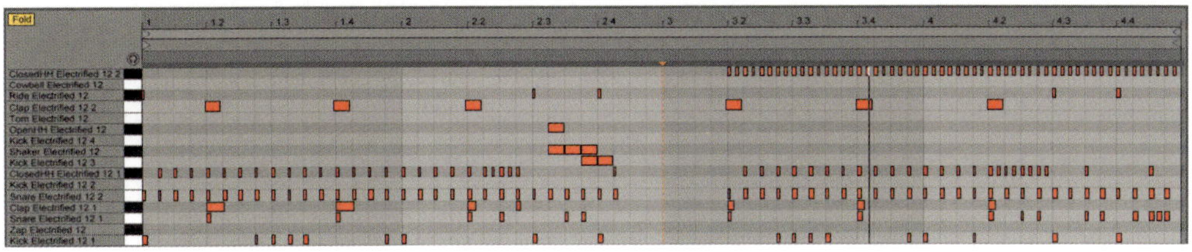

Hesitation - Conversely, try writing a drum fill that lasts longer than expected, extending over the formal boundary between the sections and ending after the rest of the musical material has already changed to the new section. In these cases, it often works well if there's no sharp emphasis on the end of the fill, and instead the drums of the new section simply take over as seamlessly as possible after the fill. Here's an example of a drum fill that hesitates beyond the sectional boundary. The energy continues through the downbeat and peaks on beat 2:

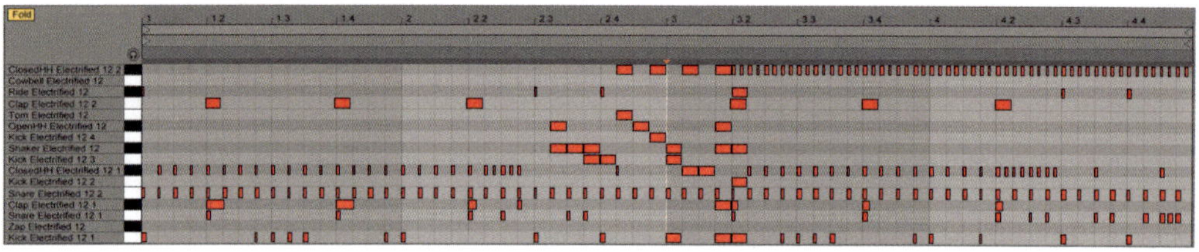

Note that you can also apply anticipation and hesitation processes to musical elements besides drums. Try embellishing bass lines using these techniques, or extending (or shortening) sustained chords.

Creating Variation 1: Mutation of Clones

Problem:

You've come up with a great-sounding seed of a musical idea. But now that you have it, you find that you don't know how to proceed. Maybe it's a few notes or a few bars, but it's definitely not long enough to be a finished piece. You keep listening to the promising idea over and over again, unable to see a direction that will get you from here to a song.

There are a number of methods for generating many new ideas from the seed of one simple idea. Here is one recipe.

Solution:

Duplicate the initial idea a number of times (maybe eight or so) so that you have a number of identical copies. Edit the first duplicate until you have made only one meaningful change. You'll ultimately need to use your own taste and intuition to determine what "meaningful" means in the context of this particular idea, but the broad categories to consider are the fundamental parameters of music:

> Sound: changes to the timbre
> Harmony: changes to the chords
> Melody: changes to the foreground line
> Rhythm: changes to the timing of events
> Form: changes to the structure or distribution of smaller-scale components within the idea

You've succeeded when you can listen to the original and the edited duplicate back-to-back and clearly hear (or at least feel) that they're somehow different.

After making your one meaningful change to the first duplicate, move to the second duplicate and again make one meaningful change. The change could be of the same type as the change you made to the previous edit or it could be a change of an entirely different musical parameter. Again, all that matters is that it is audibly different from the original (and, in this case, also audibly different from the previously edited version).

Repeat this process until you've made one meaningful change to each of the copies.

What you have now is a collection of "siblings," each of which is a direct descendant of the "parent" idea. Because you've made only one meaningful change to each duplicate, the relationship to the original will be clear.

Creating Variation 2: Mutation Over Generations

Problem:

You've come up with a great-sounding seed of a musical idea. But now that you have it, you find that you don't know how to proceed. Maybe it's a few notes or a few bars, but it's definitely not long enough to be a finished piece. You keep listening to the promising idea over and over again, unable to see a direction that will get you from here to a song.

There are a number of methods for generating many new ideas from the seed of one simple idea. Here is one recipe.

Solution:

Make a single duplicate of the initial idea. Edit this duplicate until you have made only one meaningful change. You'll ultimately need to use your own taste and intuition to determine what "meaningful" means in the context of this particular idea, but the broad categories to consider are the fundamental parameters of music:

> Sound: changes to the timbre
> Harmony: changes to the chords
> Melody: changes to the foreground line
> Rhythm: changes to the timing of events
> Form: changes to the structure or distribution of smaller-scale components within the idea

Once you're satisfied with the change that you've made to the duplicated idea, repeat the process. But this time, begin by creating a duplicate of the duplicate (rather than the original). Now make one meaningful change to this third-generation duplicate. Try not to go "backwards"; that is, don't simply undo the change that you made in the previous generation. Continue this process a number of times (maybe eight or so), each time using the previous variation as the seed for the next one.

What you have now is a collection of "descendant" ideas, each of which is the direct offspring of the previous idea, but which can all be traced back to the original "ancestor." Although you've made only one meaningful change to each idea, all of them have also inherited the changes from all of the preceding generations and so may become increasingly remote from the original ancestor.

Creating Variation 3: Note Transformations

Problem:

You've come up with a great-sounding seed of a musical idea. But now that you have it, you find that you don't know how to proceed. Maybe it's a few notes or a few bars, but it's definitely not long enough to be a finished piece. You keep listening to the promising idea over and over again, unable to see a direction that will get you from here to a song.

There are a number of methods for generating many new ideas from the seed of one simple idea. Here are some recipes.

Solution:

Most DAWs offer a range of *note transformation* features that allow you to make predictable, rule-based changes to a selection of notes. The resulting patterns will usually have a clear, organic connection to the original pattern, although they can often sound quite different. Some types of transformations include:

Transposition

Transposition means shifting an entire pattern of notes up or down by a specific number of semitones. In a transposition operation, the relationship between all of the notes in the pattern will remain unchanged. Many DAWs provide a quick way to transpose MIDI notes, but you can also do this manually by simply selecting a group of notes and dragging them vertically or horizontally to a new position on the piano roll. Transposition can also be applied to audio samples, although there will generally be some change to the timbre of the audio as a result.

Here is a one-measure-long MIDI phrase, followed by a version of that phrase that has been transposed up by five semitones:

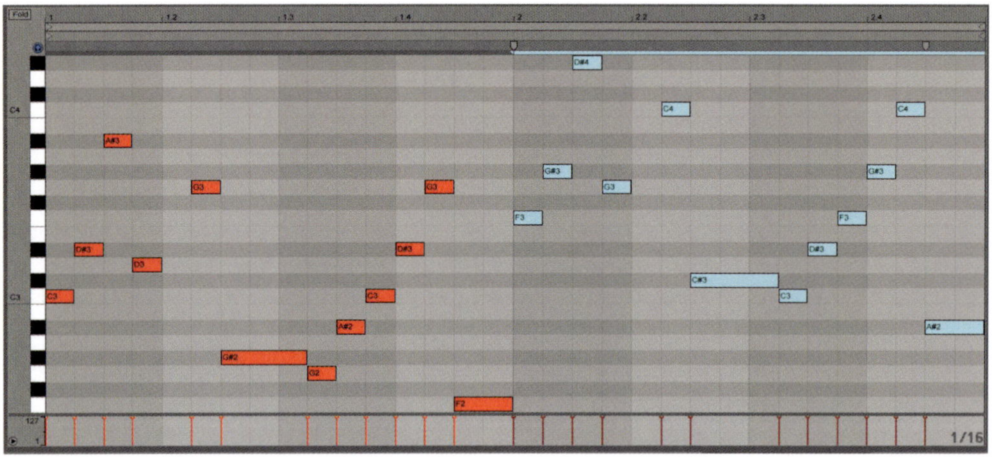

Inversion

Inversion (in this context) is the process of flipping a collection of notes "upside-down" so that the lowest note becomes the highest note and vice versa. The shape of the pattern and interval distance between each of the notes is maintained, but in the opposite direction of the original. This process can be applied in the MIDI domain, either via an automatic process built in to the DAW or by manually moving the notes. For example, here is a one-measure-long phrase, followed by a version of that phrase that has been inverted:

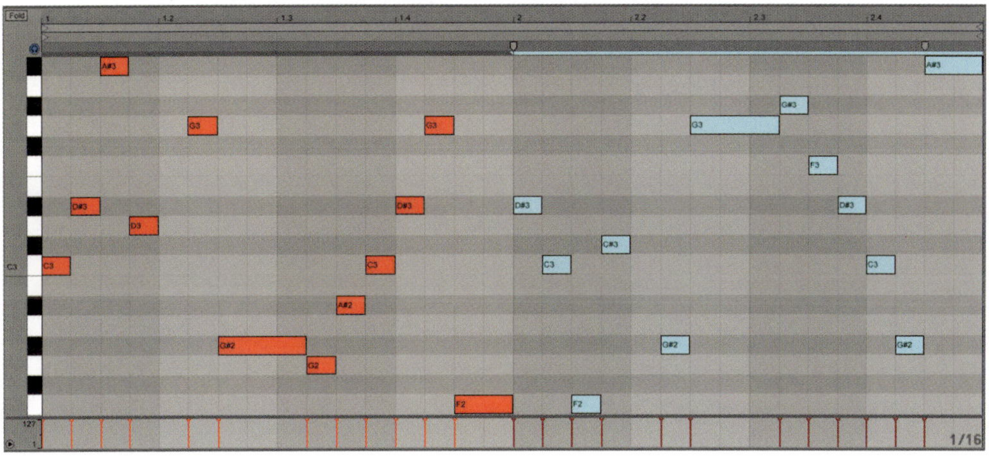

Retrograde or Reverse

Retrograde means flipping a collection of notes backwards, so that the last note becomes the first note and vice versa. This process can be applied in the MIDI domain, either via an automatic process built in to the DAW or by manually moving the notes. Retrograde can also be applied in the audio domain, usually by applying a "Reverse" function to the sample. Note, however, that reversing a sample will also reverse the envelope contour of the audio itself, so the results will be quite different than a comparable process applied to the same MIDI.

Here's an example of a one-measure-long MIDI phrase, followed by a version of that phrase that has been reversed:

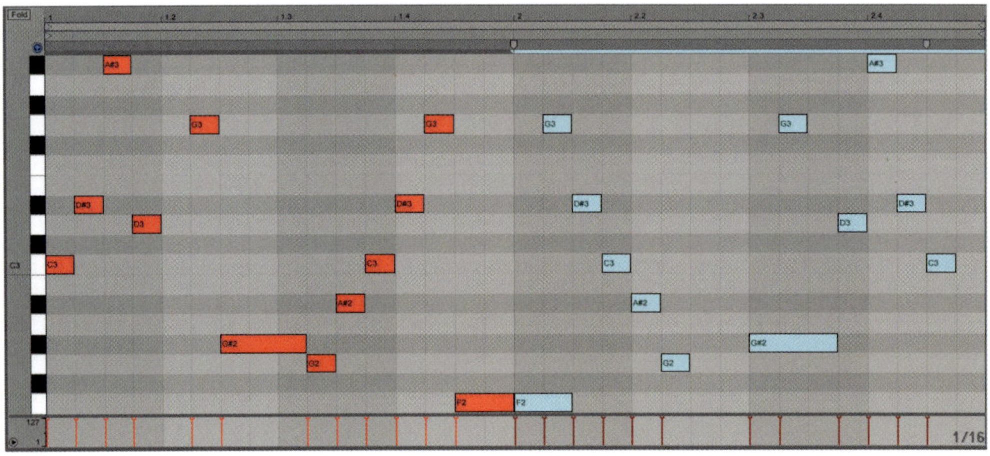

Note that in this particular retrograde algorithm, the distance between the note *onsets* is reversed. A true mirror image would mean that the note ends of the original became onsets in the reversed version. While literal mirroring is probably easier to understand conceptually, the results are often not particularly musically interesting.

Constraint to a Scale

A passage of MIDI notes can be selectively transposed so that the resulting pattern contains only notes that are within a particular scale. Many DAWs provide some type of device specifically for this purpose. These devices analyze incoming MIDI notes and remap them to an arbitrary pool of available notes before sending them out again.

Here's an example of a one-measure-long MIDI phrase containing a somewhat random collection of notes, followed by a version of that phrase that has been constrained to the pitches within the C Major scale:

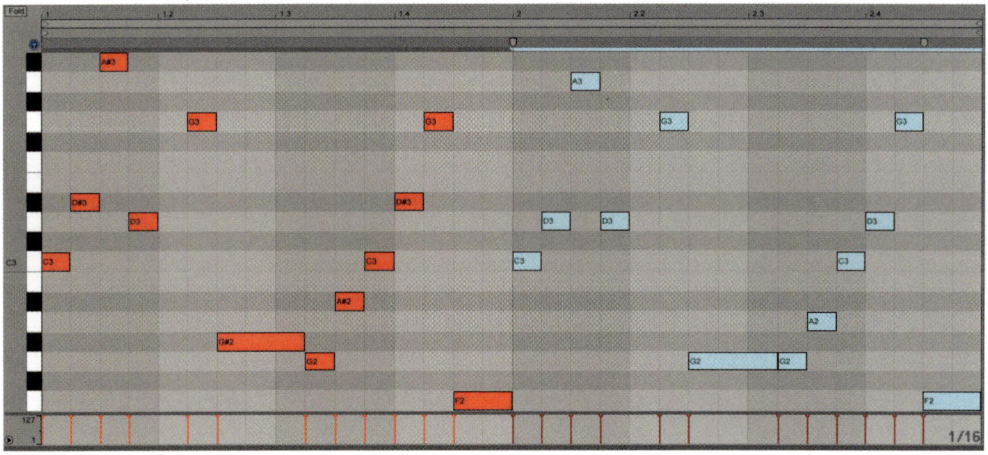

Although the example above shows the actual notes that result from a scale-constraint process, note that many DAWs with MIDI processing devices apply their processing after the notes in the clip.

In order to get the notes you hear back into the original clip (as in the previous example), follow these steps:

1. Create a new MIDI track and set up your DAW's inter-track routing so that the new track records the output of the original track.
2. Copy the newly-recorded notes to the clipboard.
3. Paste them back into the original clip.
4. Disable or remove the scale-constraint device.

Time Shifting

A looped passage of material can be started at an arbitrary position within the passage. This is effectively the same as maintaining the exact pitches and rhythms of the original pattern, but shifting the pattern right or left to a new location. Some DAWs allow you to adjust the playback start position for a particular pattern independently of any other patterns. In these environments, simply moving the pattern's start position achieves this effect. Here's an example of our original one-bar pattern with its start marker shifted three sixteenth notes to the right:

In other DAWs, you can manually copy the entire pattern and paste it to the new location with the desired offset. When shifting to the right, keep in mind that material near the end of the original pattern will need to be "wrapped around" to the beginning of the new pattern, and vice versa when shifting to the left.

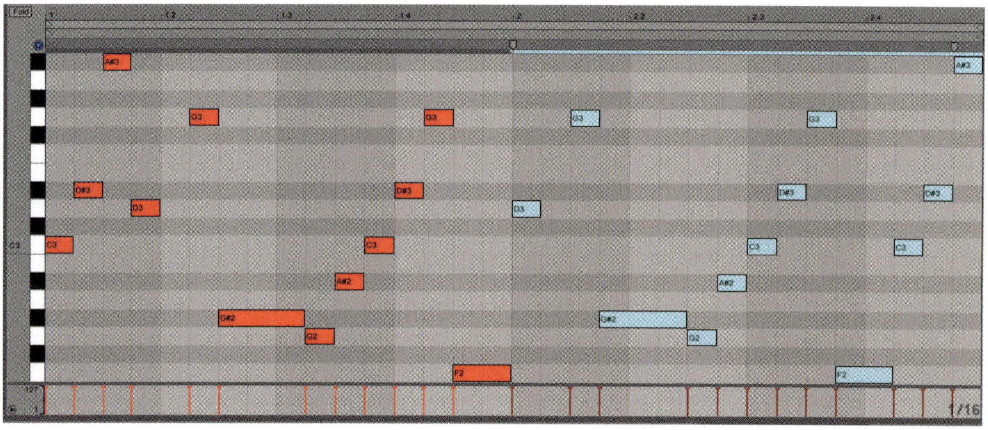

Pitch Rotation

Pitch rotation is a process whereby the rhythm of a passage of notes is retained but the pitches from the passage are shifted to the right or left in time. Here's an example of a one-measure-long MIDI phrase, followed by a version of that phrase that has been rotated to the right by three pitches. As with time shifting, pitches near the end of the pattern will need to be "wrapped around" to the beginning of the new pattern, and vice versa when shifting to the left.

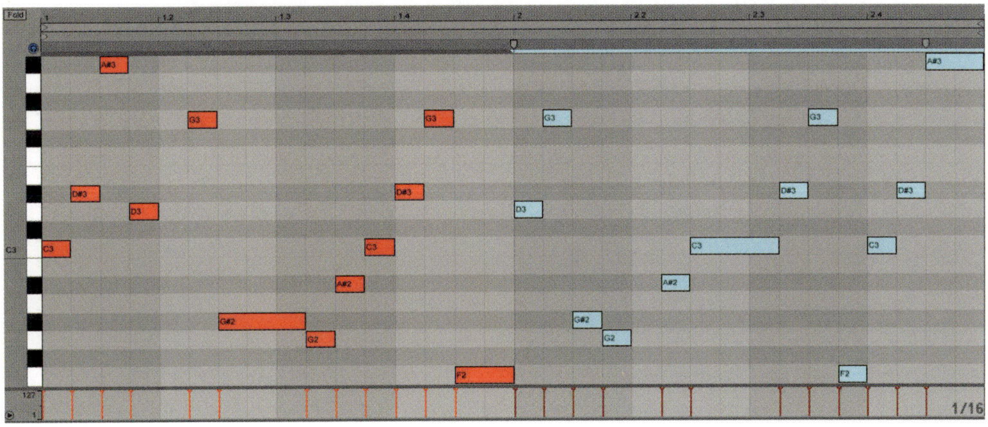

More Ways to Use the Transformations

Note that in all of these examples, the transformed version occurs immediately after the original. But of course, you could also treat the transformed version as an entirely separate, isolated pattern. Conversely, you could also overlap the transformation with the original to create a more complex pattern:

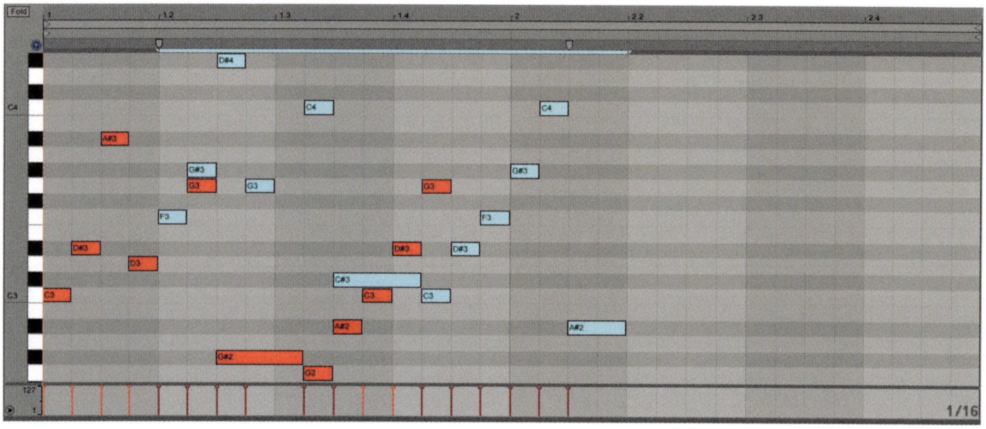

Or you could even superimpose them completely to create harmony:

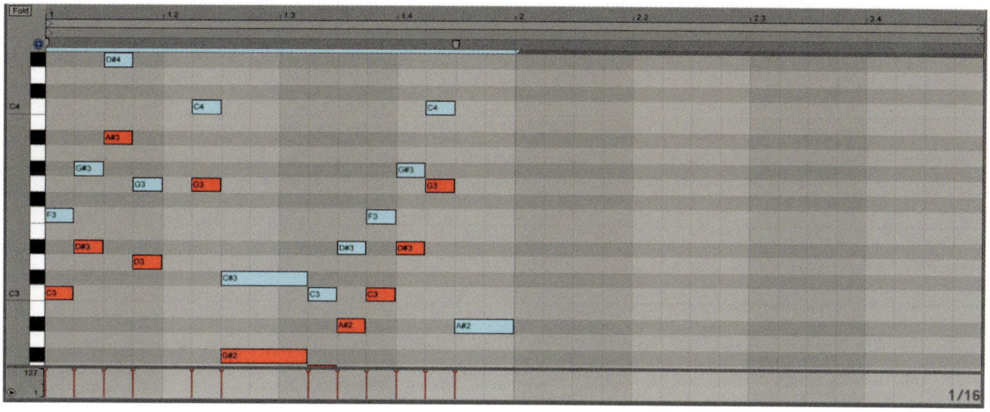

Implied Rhythm in Short Loops

Problem:

You keep making the same kinds of beats over and over again, and you're looking for a way to expand your palette of rhythmic ideas.

We often develop a "vocabulary" of musical ideas that we rely on to create new music. Like spoken language, the richness of our musical expression is directly related to the depth of this vocabulary. When we know only a few words, we can say only a few things. Likewise, when we know only a few musical patterns, we're limited in our ability to create music that's different from the last time.

The most obvious place to get ideas for new beats is from other music, but here's an idea for finding rhythms in another way.

Solution:

Find or make an audio recording of anything. You'll get the best results from material that has at least some variation over time; a steady-state sine wave probably won't work well for our purposes here, but almost anything else is a viable source. It should be at least a few seconds long, but beyond this there are no restrictions on length. Very long material—minutes, hours, etc.—is fine.

Import this audio into your DAW and create a loop around an arbitrary portion of it. Now, while listening, begin to decrease the length of the loop until it's at most a few seconds long. One- or two-second loops seem to work best for this exercise.

As you continue to listen carefully to this loop for a while, you'll start to notice rhythmic patterns emerge. These are the result of our inherent ability to find patterns in chaos, like hearing the sound of a ringing phone in the white noise of a shower. The phenomenon of finding patterns in unordered stimulus is known as *pareidolia*. For example, most people see a "face" in this image of a natural rock formation on Mars.

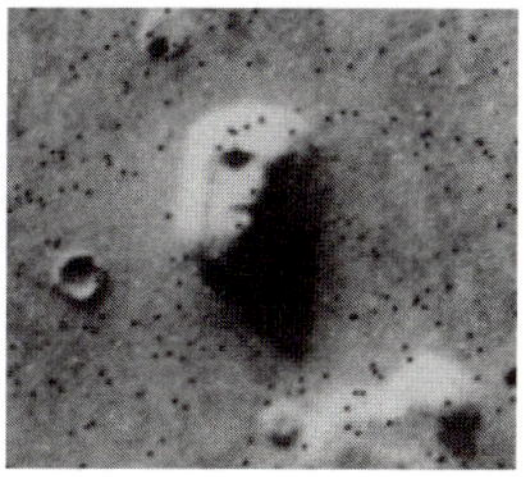

The bits and pieces of sound that make up the perceived rhythmic patterns may be the result of technical "errors" in your sample playback tool, such as loop boundaries that aren't aligned with zero-crossing points in the sample. For our purposes here, these errors are exactly what we want; don't try to fix them by enabling features with names like "snap to zero-crossings."

If your original source material already had a clearly defined rhythm or tempo, try to loop a portion of the material that plays against this in a clearly audible way. For example, make the loop so that the repetitions are not synchronized with the original tempo. The goal isn't to make use of the overt rhythms that exist in the large-scale source material, but rather to discover the rhythms that emerge from the repetition of tiny portions.

Good sources include:

> Existing music (ideally by you or by someone from whom you've secured rights, but anything can work technically). Remember, however, that you're not looking for the musical information from the original source. The goal is to find the implied rhythm heard only when listening repeatedly to tiny fragments.

> Field recordings of any kind—urban, industrial, or nature sounds work quite well for this.

> Recordings of speech. Rhythmic patterns emerge quite naturally from repeated fragments of speech. In fact, melodic patterns tend to emerge from short speech loops as well. For an interesting example of this in practice, listen to Steve Reich's *Different Trains* for string quartet and tape. For this piece, Reich listened for the implied melodies in short fragments of speech and then transcribed them to be played by the stringed instruments.

~ *Bonus:* In addition to audio, you can also use this technique with your own MIDI recordings, particularly if you've recorded extended improvised material without a metronome. Again, try to adjust the loop so that it plays against any rhythm or tempo that's suggested by the original material itself.

Once these rhythms have emerged from the loop, there are several different ways you can proceed. The most obvious is to simply use the looped sample as an element in your song. For an interesting example of this, listen to Machinedrum's "Baby It's U" from the album *Vapor City*, which uses hydrophone recordings of dolphins and shrimp as both the basis of the groove and as a rhythmic backdrop over which more conventional drums are eventually added. Another solution is to apply the emergent rhythms from the original sample to another instrument, as in the previously mentioned string quartet *Different Trains*.

Asynchronous or Polyrhythmic Loops

Problem:

Many electronic genres make extensive use of loops. When you listen to your favorite examples of loop-based music, there's always some sense of motion that keeps the music fresh and interesting, but your own attempts to work this way usually strike you as static and boring.

It seems like a paradox, but "simple"-sounding loop-based genres like minimal techno can be difficult to emulate. All of the elements are on the surface, and it's easy to hear through the few layers of production. But although the surface level of much of this music suggests that there isn't much happening, there's a subtlety and richness of detail at work that separates the good music from the bad.

Our typical mental model of a sequenced MIDI loop in a DAW is something like this: An instrument is played by one looping clip with a fixed length (probably equal to one or more complete bars). At some point, we might stop this clip and then start another clip in its place. So at any moment, any given instrument is either silent or is being triggered by one clip.

Here's a different way of thinking about looped clips that might make things more interesting.

Solution:

Instead of triggering an instrument with a single clip, try simultaneously triggering it with multiple clips of different lengths. In most DAWs, this will require some kind of inter-track routing. For example, one track could contain the instrument, while one or more additional tracks contain no instruments but instead only the clips that will play the instrument on the first track. These "silent" clips will then have their output routed to the first track.

In this example, imagine an instrument is triggered by a simple looping MIDI pattern consisting of four sixteenth notes:

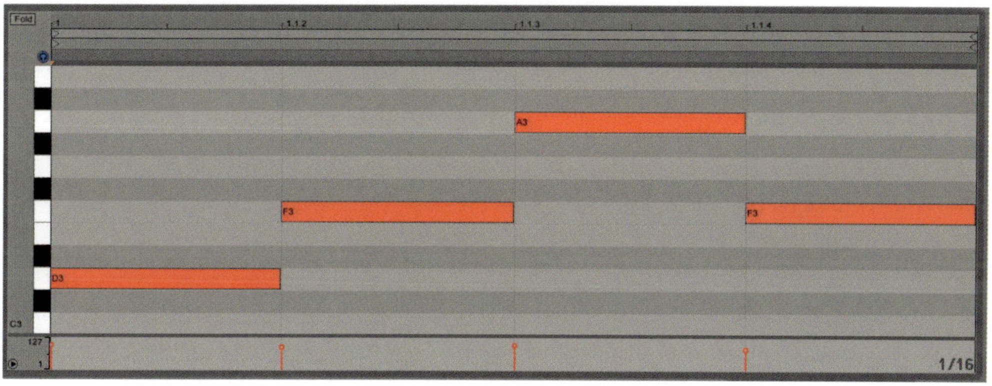

Simultaneously, the same instrument is being triggered by another loop that contains one sixteenth note followed by four sixteenths of silence. This pattern loops every five sixteenths; it is one sixteenth longer than the first pattern, so they will play out of sync with each other but in time with a shared pulse, a phenomenon known as *polyrhythm*.

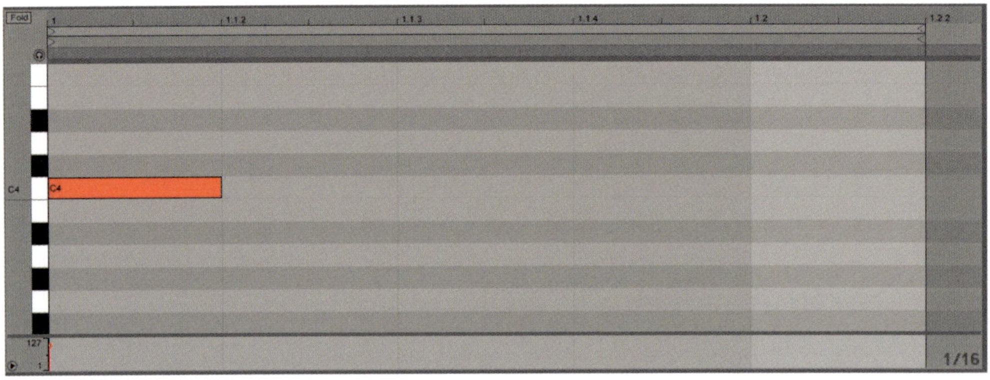

The simultaneous juxtaposition of these two patterns creates an interesting auditory phenomenon. The ear can now hear three simultaneous patterns: the two that are actually being played and the resulting composite, which finally comes back into sync every 20 sixteenth notes:

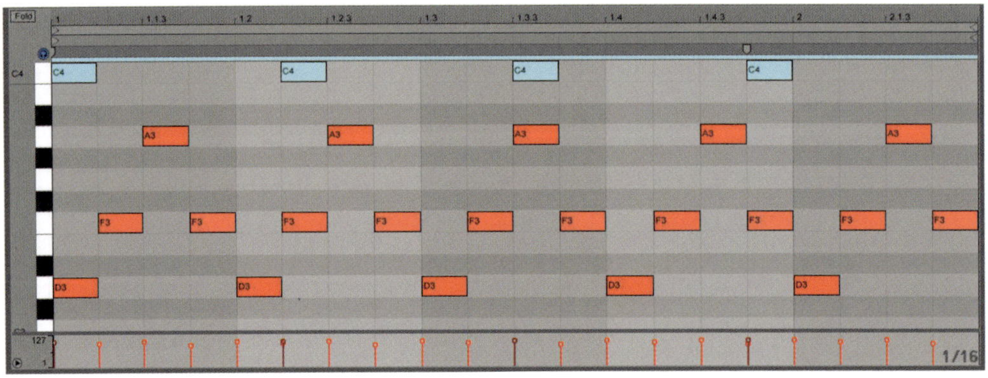

Here are some variations on these concepts:

> Try adding more loops of differing lengths. For example, adding a third loop to the earlier example that repeats every three sixteenth notes will create a composite that is three times as long; the original patterns will realign after 60 sixteenth notes.

> Rather than letting the composite naturally realign, you could "artificially" realign it anywhere in an arrangement by simply pasting the clips so they begin at that point.

> Some DAWs allow automation to loop at a length that is "unlinked" from the length of the notes in the clip. For example, you could create an envelope that varies a synthesizer's filter cutoff and have this envelope loop at yet another length from the loops containing notes. Even if your DAW doesn't have this functionality within clips, you could manually create repeating automation patterns of any length when you build your arrangement.

> Similarly, if you have some kind of modulation source that can control parameters (like an LFO, for example), you could set this to a rate which is again asynchronous in relation to the looping notes.

> If you're using a plug-in instrument, try using duplicates of the instrument with slightly altered timbres, rather than actually using the exact same instrument. This will weaken the sense of a single composite pattern but may be more interesting anyway. You could even use this technique with hardware synths, provided you have enough of them (or you're willing to bounce to audio after recording each pattern separately).

> When set against other instruments that are playing in more standard loop lengths, even a single "odd" loop can create the same kind of interesting effects. This approach is common in a lot of early acid tracks; listen to almost anything by Hardfloor for examples.

Layering of simultaneous asynchronous loops is a common hallmark of the so-called "Berlin School" of electronic music from the 70s and 80s, which was largely defined by multiple modular sequencers, each playing a monophonic loop consisting of a different number of notes.

A similar technique can be found in ambient pieces such as Brian Eno's *Music for Airports*, which is made from multiple tape loops of different lengths. This "analog" approach to the concept is truly asynchronous—if played forever, uneven tape loops are unlikely to ever resynchronize. You could achieve a similar effect in your DAW by offsetting one of your loop lengths so that it's not quite aligned to the metric grid. Try playing with the amount of offset until you find relationships which sound interesting. This can create some very unusual rhythmic effects.

Misusing Rhythmic Tools

Problem:

You have a variety of tools in your DAW arsenal—such as quantization, slicing, and beat-juggling effects—that are designed to help you work with rhythmic material. But you feel like there's more potential in these tools that you haven't yet discovered.

Some workflows and effects are clearly designed for use with very specific types of material. But there's no reason why you can't repurpose them for other uses. Here are some ideas for how to creatively misuse rhythmic tools to achieve unexpected results.

Solutions:

Misusing Quantization

Quantization is typically used to correct timing errors in manually played MIDI material and, in some DAWs, audio samples. But there are a number of ways to use quantization “incorrectly,” sometimes with surprising results.

One interesting experiment: Try quantizing to a note value that is substantially slower or faster than the source material. If you played sixteenth notes, for example, try quantizing to a slower note value like quarter notes. If you originally played a monophonic figure, you'll end up generating chords. You can even apply successively larger quantization values to already quantized material to achieve the same effect. Here's a figure played in sixteenth notes:

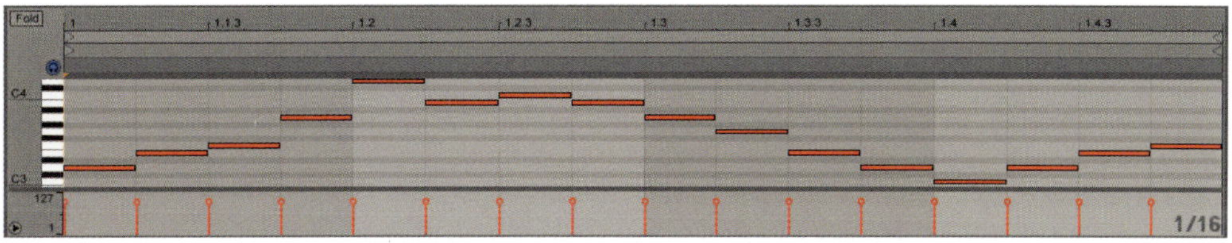

And here's the same material after quantizing to quarter notes:

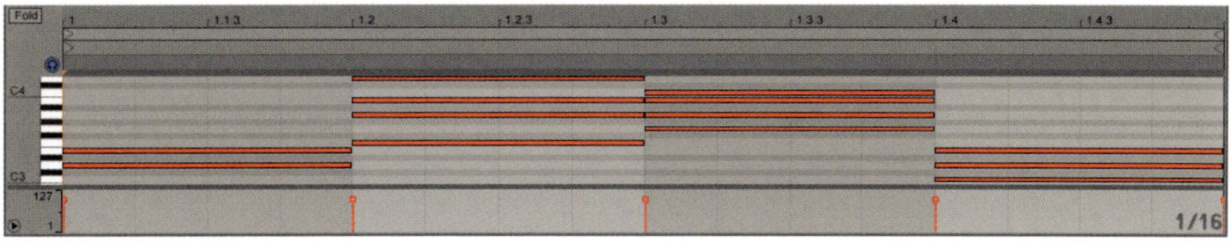

Another way to generate unexpected results from quantization is to start by playing your parts at a dramatically faster tempo than you actually intend. Because the errors in your playing will likely be more extreme than usual, applying quantization will then "correct" the note placements to unusual positions. When you then slow the tempo down to a more musically appropriate one, you may have created patterns that you never would have played intentionally.

Misusing Slicing

Slicing is typically used to separate rhythmic events (such as drum hits) from audio material such as drum beats or bass lines. But there's no reason why you can't slice any audio material, including entirely ambient pads, field recordings, or other non-rhythmic samples.

Another idea: If your DAW allows you to create or move markers in the original audio to determine the positions at which slices will be created, try placing the markers in deliberately "wrong" places.

In many DAWs, slicing generates a new instrument—and potentially a new effects chain—for each slice. This makes it easy to apply dramatically different types of processing to individual slices, regardless of their source. For this reason, slicing can often lead to interesting results even when you're slicing things in the "wrong" ways.

Misusing Beat-Juggling Effects

Effects that chop and rearrange incoming audio material in real time are normally used for creating variations of beats. But, as with the slicing examples discussed previously, you can also create interesting results by feeding these effects with any other material, including things that have no clear rhythm at all.

Although these are some examples for how to misuse specific workflows, consider applying this approach to all of your tools. Any effect, instrument, or workflow can potentially yield interesting results when used in unusual ways. Learn what your tools are supposed to do, but don't be afraid to make them do something else.

3+3+2 Rhythm

Problem:

There's a particular off-kilter, asymmetrical, funky rhythm that you keep hearing in music of all kinds, from hip-hop to footwork to rock and roll. What is it, and how can you use it in your own music?

For new producers, there's a tendency to be overwhelmed by the perception that all music is radically unique. The reality, however, is that there is a shared vocabulary of underlying musical patterns that artists frequently reuse across a variety of genres. Here's one of the most common.

Solution:

The *tresillo*, or 3+3+2 pattern, is a widely used rhythmic pattern. Its origins are unknown, but it's a staple of African and Latin music and was eventually incorporated into early jazz, after which it made its way to all of jazz's descendants: R&B, rock, funk, and eventually modern electronic music. In its simplest form, the 3+3+2 pattern looks like this:

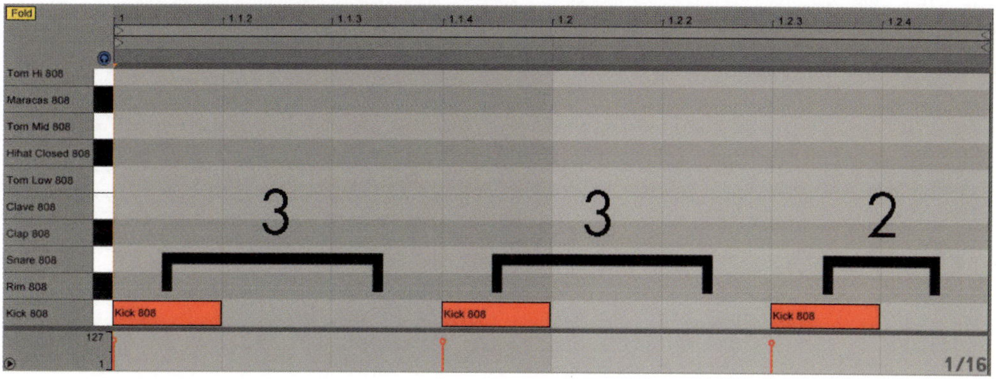

The "3+3+2" refers to the number of sixteenth notes between hits, and the pattern repeats every two beats. The pattern can also be played with other note durations; a half-time version would be measured in eighth notes, for example, and would repeat every four beats.

As a stand-alone pattern, 3+3+2 might not be so useful, but it really becomes interesting when overlaid against other patterns that are more symmetrical. For example, here's the previous example as a kick drum pattern underlying a basic rock groove and expanded to fill a full bar:

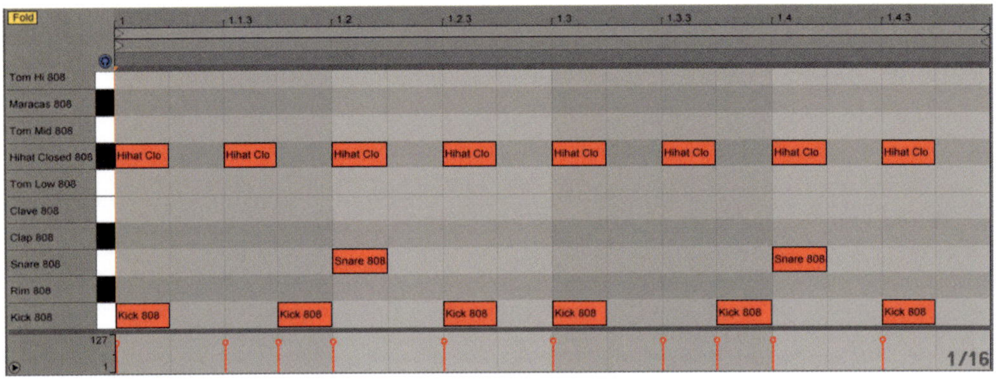

If the backbeats occur at half the speed (on beat 3 rather than beats 2 and 4), this same pattern begins to resemble a simplified version of the drum programming heard in a lot of bass music. With the addition of hi-hats on the offbeat eighth notes, the drum part for the track "No Think" by Sepalcure is based off this basic pattern:

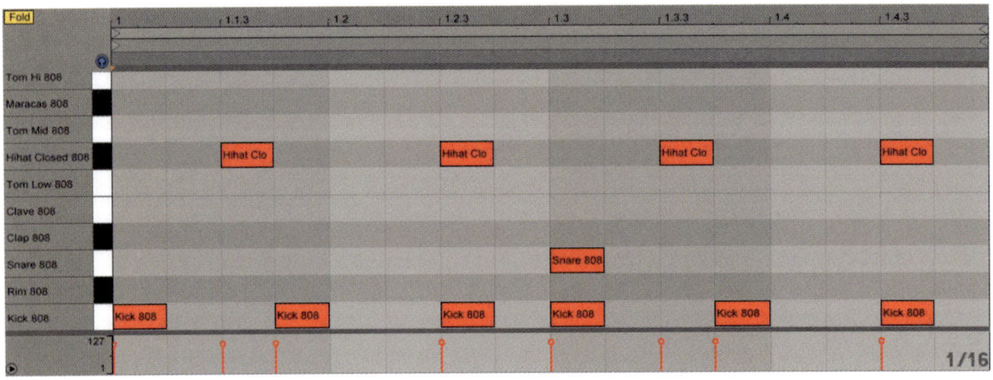

As you can see, there is a huge range of possibilities available just by combining the standard 3+3+2 rhythm with various other rhythms. Additionally, there are a number of ways to subtly vary the basic pattern, which can yield even more possibilities.

Skipping or adding one or more notes. By leaving out certain notes of the pattern, you can maintain the syncopation and asymmetry but in a more subtle way. Conversely, by adding notes to the pattern, you can create an embellished version. The main drum pattern in Lil Jon's "Turn Down for What" is an example of both processes at work. This is a four-bar phrase in which the kick drum pattern consists of three different types of 3+3+2 pattern:

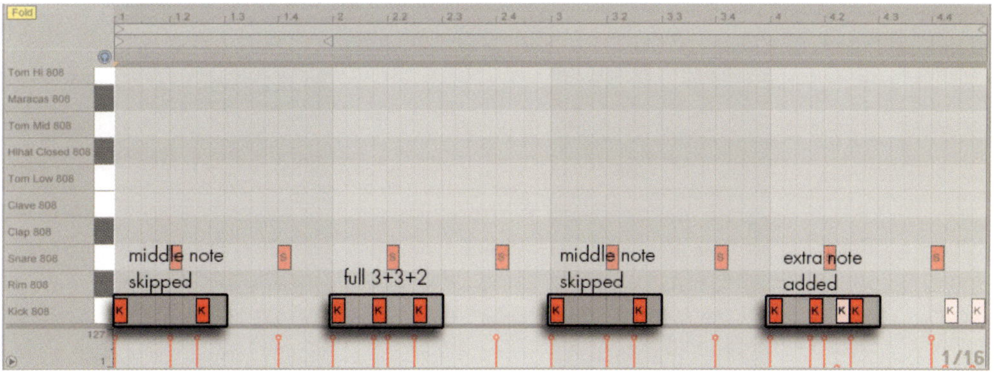

The first and third phrases are identical, with the middle "3" of the 3+3+2 left unplayed. The second and fourth phrases play the whole pattern, but the fourth also adds an additional sixteenth immediately before the final "2." But because the 3+3+2 pattern has already been so strongly established, we hear this note purely as an ornament; the underlying 3+3+2 is still dominant.

Extending the "3." The "2" portion of the 3+3+2 pattern serves to resynchronize the gesture with the metric grid. But very interesting things can happen if you delay this resynchronization by repeating the "3" parts of the gesture additional times. An example of this can be heard in the track "Tenderly" by Disclosure. Here, the two-bar kick and clap pattern looks like this:

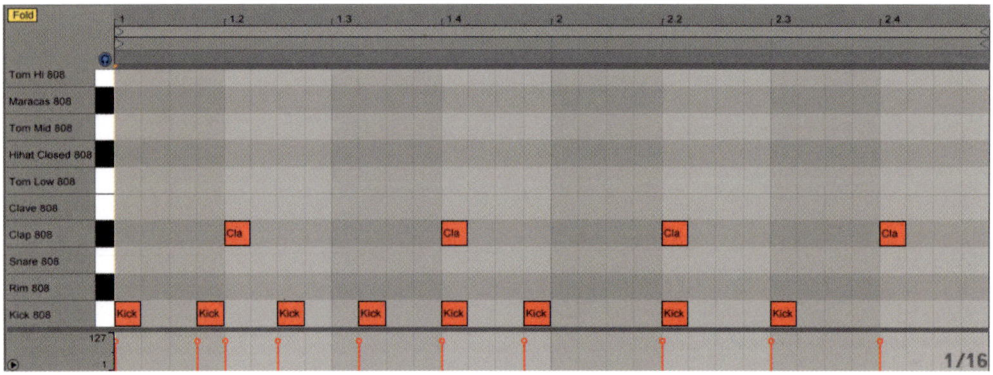

There are six kick drums in the first bar, which are all three sixteenths apart, followed by a pause and then a clear "realignment" with kicks on beats two and three in the second bar. This creates a strong contrast between rhythmic stability and instability, tension and release.

Now that you're familiar with the 3+3+2 rhythm, you'll start to notice it in various forms in all sorts of different kinds of music. And it's not just useful for drum patterns. You can use 3+3+2 to build bass lines, chords, and melodies as well.

Programming Beats 1: On Looseness

Problem:

Your programmed drum beats just don't have the right feel. When you play them in by hand, they sound sloppy. But when you program them with the mouse or by quantizing your manual playing, they sound too perfect.

In certain genres of electronic music (like some techno, house, electro, and EDM) absolute quantization is completely appropriate for the style. It's common to hear drum parts in these styles with both perfect timing and completely consistent and unvarying dynamics. But for other styles (like most hip-hop), a looser, more organic feel is often more appropriate. In much of this music, drum parts are often directly sampled from recordings of real drummers. So in songs where programmed drums are desired instead, it often makes sense to try to emulate the human feel that comes naturally to actual humans. But while humanness isn't a characteristic that comes naturally to machines, many beat programmers don't have the drumming skills to program convincing drum parts that sound like something a real drummer would play. Here are some ideas that can help you with your beat programming, whether you're a drummer or not.

Solutions:

Apply Quantization in Small Amounts

Most modern DAWs provide controls that allow you to change the intensity or amount of quantization applied, usually represented as a percentage. For example, if you're quantizing to sixteenth notes at 100% quantization, the selected notes will be moved forward or backward from their current position to the nearest sixteenth note. But quantizing to 50% will move the notes only half of the distance between their original position and the nearest "correct" note position. This means that human inaccuracies will be reduced rather than eliminated. This technique is probably the best way to retain a sense of human feel while still allowing you to correct for some sloppiness in your playing.

Apply Quantization to Only Certain Instruments

After recording a drum pattern with a MIDI controller, the typical approach is to apply quantization to the entire pattern, which means that all of the instruments in the drum kit will be shifted as a single unit. Instead of this, try selecting and quantizing only some of the instruments in the kit, leaving the others exactly as you played them. For example, try quantizing only the hi-hats, leaving the kick and snare alone. Or try the inverse, leaving the hi-hats loose but quantizing the kick and snare so that they're perfectly in time. Although any perfect quantization is not really a representation of how a real drummer would play, this technique can result in much more realistic-sounding drum patterns. You can also combine this technique with the previous one for even more possibilities.

Find Your "Natural" Tempo

A common technique when programming drum patterns in real time is to record at a slow tempo and then increase the tempo during playback. While it's true that it may be easier to play accurately at slower tempos, there's usually a bottom limit to this, and most drummers (and non-drummers) find that their rhythm is most accurate within a particular range of tempos—not too slow, and not too fast. This range varies from person to person however, and if you hope to improve your beat programming, experiment to find the tempos that work best for you. Once you've found something that feels comfortable, try programming your beats here and see if you can get the feel you want without applying any quantization afterwards. Keep in mind that timing errors are generally more perceptible if you play back at a slower tempo than you recorded, and less perceptible if you play back faster.

Humanize/Randomize

In addition to adjusting how much you quantize after recording, you can also sometimes get very musical results by applying "humanization" (subtle timing and/or velocity randomization) to your material. Even if you've quantized something to lock completely to the grid, humanization provides a way to reverse this effect, placing notes some distance away from the quantized positions according to whatever algorithm your DAW uses for this process. Note that applying randomization to material that *hasn't* been quantized will likely just exaggerate any timing inaccuracies that were already there; this process usually works best with material that's exactly on the grid.

Adjusting Velocity Instead Of/In Addition to Timing

Although timing is the most important variable that determines the feel of drum patterns, the relative volumes (velocities) of individual notes can also have a significant effect. For example, a hi-hat pattern in straight sixteenth notes sounds quite different if all of the velocities are identical than it does if there is some variation in volume from note to note. Most drummers will play a pattern like this with a slight emphasis on the first and third sixteenths, while playing slightly quieter on the second and fourth:

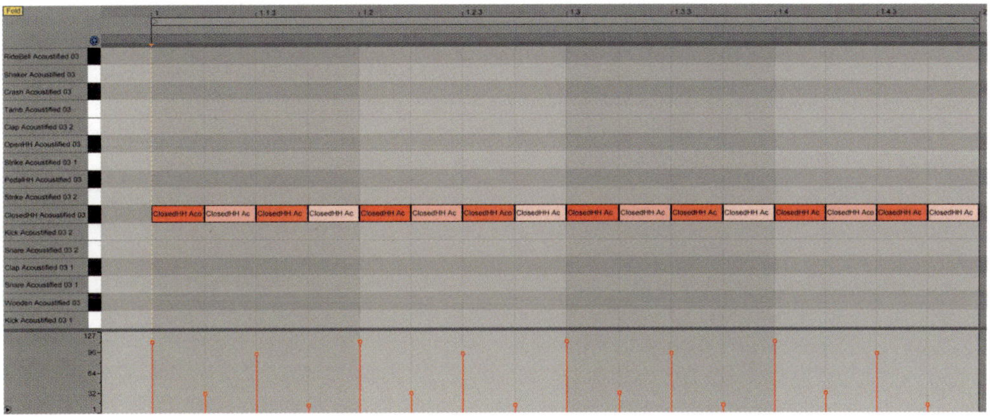

The image above shows a hi-hat pattern with perfect quantization but with velocities similar to what a drummer might play. Even without adjusting timing at all, you can often make a stiff, static groove come to life by carefully adjusting some of the velocities.

Manually Shift Specific Elements

Both for quantized and unquantized material, the surefire way to get the results you want is also the most time-consuming. Manually editing individual notes to change their relationship to each other and to the metric grid can ensure that everything happens exactly where you want it. Unfortunately, this assumes that you know what you're looking for, which may not be the case. Here are some ideas:

> Try dragging some or all of the snare drum or hi-hat notes slightly after their "intended" grid positions to create a heavy or "laid-back" feel. You'll often hear this "behind the beat" approach in funk drumming. Here's an example of hi-hats placed slightly after the beat:

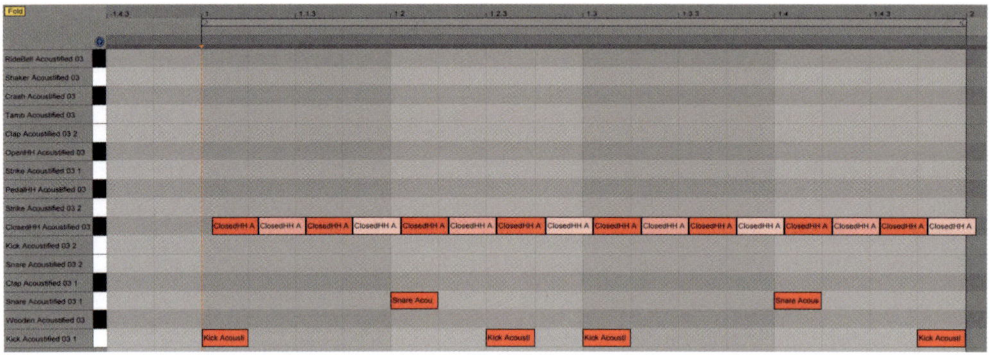

> Conversely, placing them early can make the music sound nervous or "driving forward." You'll often hear ska or punk drummers play "ahead of the beat." Here's an example of hi-hats placed slightly before the beat. Note that the "first" note has been moved to the end of the pattern, so that it plays slightly before the loop point.

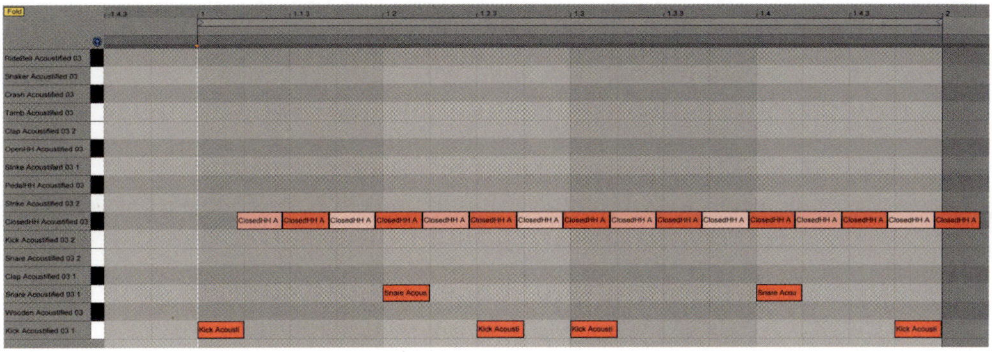

How far to move the notes is entirely up to you; there's no formula for this. Very small shifts tend to work well at slower tempos, while you'll need to make more drastic changes as the tempo increases. But in general, even a little bit of distance from the grid can be very effective.

Keep in mind that if you move *every* instrument together, the listener won't hear any change. These subtle shifts are only audible if they occur in relation to other elements that have not been moved.

Programming Beats 2: Linear Drumming

Problem:

Your programmed drum beats tend to use the available instruments in "expected" ways: Hi-hats keep time, kick drums emphasize the beats, snares/claps are placed on or around the backbeats (beats 2 and 4). But in the music you admire, you sometimes hear other, more creative ways of working with drums. Sometimes it almost sounds like the drums are playing a "melody" of their own. But when you try to create patterns like this, it just sounds random and chaotic.

The various instruments in a drum kit have a tendency to be used in a somewhat standardized way. This is true across a variety of genres, both acoustic and electronic. For example, here's a very basic rock and roll drum pattern:

The kick drum plays on every beat, the snare on the backbeats, and the hi-hats on every eighth note.

This can be converted into a very basic house pattern simply by removing all of the hi-hat notes that appear on strong beats (leaving only the offbeat eighth notes):

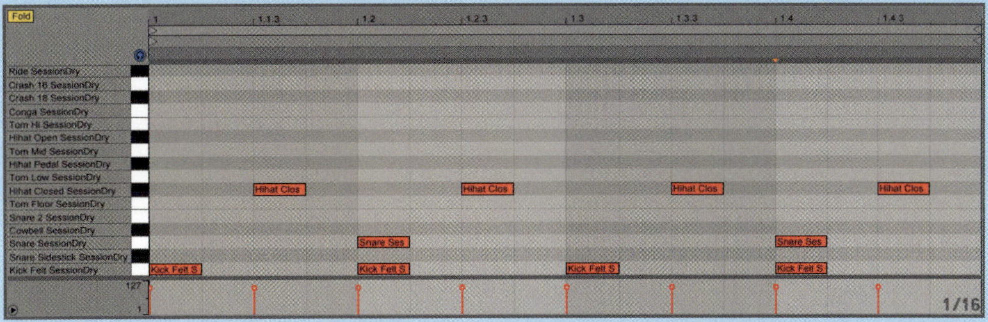

One of the hallmarks of these kinds of conventional drum patterns is that they're *polyphonic*—multiple instruments can play at the same time. For a human drummer with four limbs, there's a maximum possible polyphony of four simultaneous "voices." Of course in the electronic realm, there's no such limitation, although experienced drum programmers who are working in styles that are meant to mimic acoustic drums will generally stick with this four-voice limitation in order to create parts that sound as realistic as possible.

A side effect of thinking about drum patterns as polyphonic textures is that we tend to treat at least one layer as unvarying. In the grooves discussed earlier, for example, note that each individual instrument maintains a symmetrical pattern that never changes. In many musical contexts, these kinds of simple, steady patterns are completely appropriate. But here's another way of writing drum patterns that can yield some interesting results.

Solution:

Acoustic drummers (particularly in some funk, R&B, and fusion contexts) sometimes use a type of playing called *linear drumming*. This simply means monophonic—no two instruments can play at the same time. Linear drumming is similar to the melodic technique called hocket (see Linear Rhythm in Melodies (page 224)). An extremely simple linear drumming pattern derived from the previous examples might look like this:

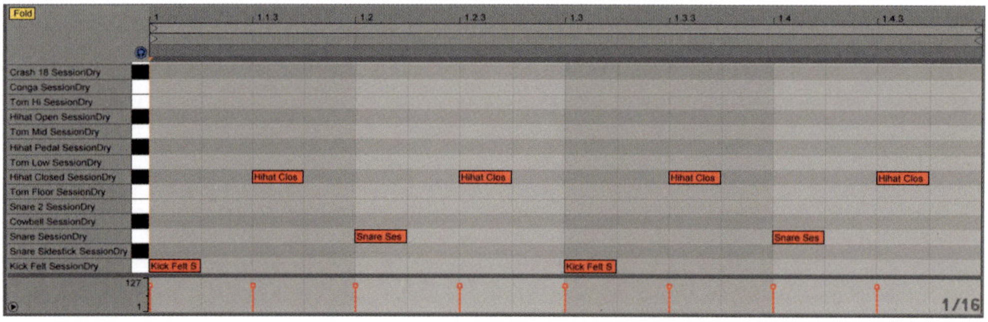

But rather than just taking a conventional pattern and removing overlapping elements, try thinking about how to use the monophonic requirement in creative ways. For example, treating a monophonic drum part as a single, quasi-melodic line of notes may cause you to think of each instrument as having the same level of importance, rather than subconsciously assigning them to functional roles (like "timekeeping" or "accenting"). Consider the following pattern:

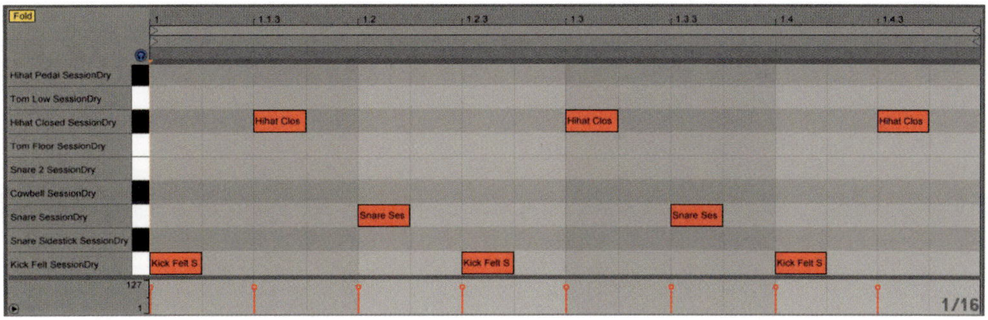

In the above pattern, sub-patterns in groups of three notes play against the expected flow of time, before "correcting" with a two-note pattern at the end of the measure.

These types of unusual note groupings treat each instrument as equally weighted, rather than using the overlaying of multiple voices to emphasize particular beat positions. Interestingly, patterns like this tend to be perceived very differently at different tempos. At a fast tempo such as 170 bpm, this pattern takes on a "rolling" character, and the composite line—the perceived fusing of the separate parts—becomes much more audible in relation to the individual notes. Linear patterns like this are common in drum and bass grooves, for example.

It's also potentially interesting to add an additional level of restriction. You might decide, for example, that your pattern will be based entirely on sixteenth notes, and that every sixteenth-note position on the grid must contain a note. A complex two-measure version of such a pattern might look like this:

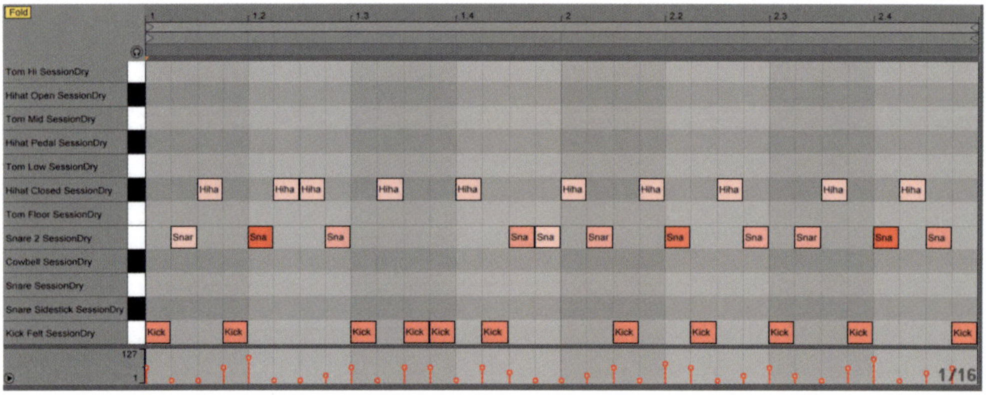

As with the previous pattern, the linear approach here helps to "democratize" the instruments. No one voice has dominance over the others, and the traditional roles of timekeeping elements vs. accenting element are eliminated. Also, notice that there's a lot of variation in note velocities in this example. Just by changing the volume of certain notes in relation to the others, you can make a single pattern of notes take on an entirely different character.

Linear drum patterns aren't right for every musical context, but they can offer a different way of thinking about beat programming that may help you come up with new patterns and variations that you might otherwise not have considered. And of course, as with all of the suggestions in this book, there's no reason to restrict yourself to strictly following the monophonic requirement. If a linear pattern would sound better with some instances of multiple simultaneous voices, go ahead and use them.

Programming Beats 3: Ghost Notes

Problem:

You're listening to a lot of acoustic drummers to get ideas for how to program more realistic drum parts, and you keep hearing very quiet sounds in between what are the clearly important hits. These are barely audible but still somehow sound intentional. And most importantly, they seem to make the groove work better. What are these sounds, and how can you use them in your own music?

In a lot of "purely" electronic music, there is often little to no variation in dynamics between notes played by a single instrument or even between all of the instruments. Each kick drum, clap, snare, etc. is generally triggered at the same volume. While this makes sense in many genres, it's quite different from how human drummers play, and if you're interested in making your drum parts sound more human, it may help to incorporate a technique drummers call *ghost notes*.

Solution:

Ghost notes are *extremely* quiet notes, normally played on the snare drum, that help to fill in the space between the prominent notes in the pattern. Ghost notes are nearly (but not completely) silent and are generally played as quietly as possible (although this varies in practice and between genres). For example, here's a basic one-bar rock drum pattern played without ghost notes:

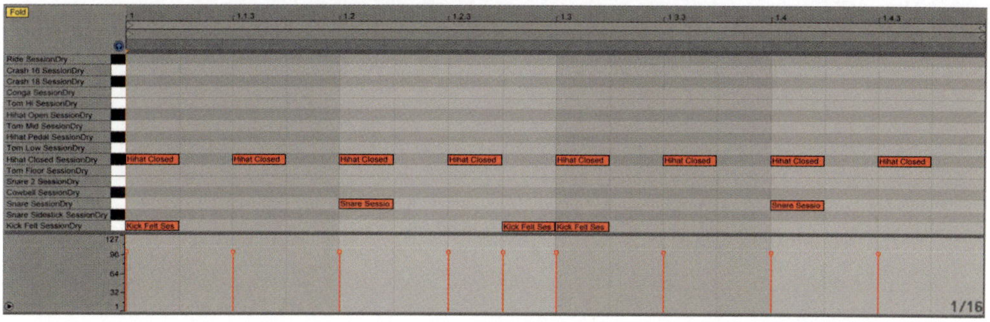

The hi-hat provides the regular "timekeeping" function, while the kick and snare provide accents that orient the listener to the place within the bar. This works fine and might be perfect for many musical situations. But in some cases, it might sound better if there's a bit more activity in between the snare backbeats.

A drummer might play the pattern like this:

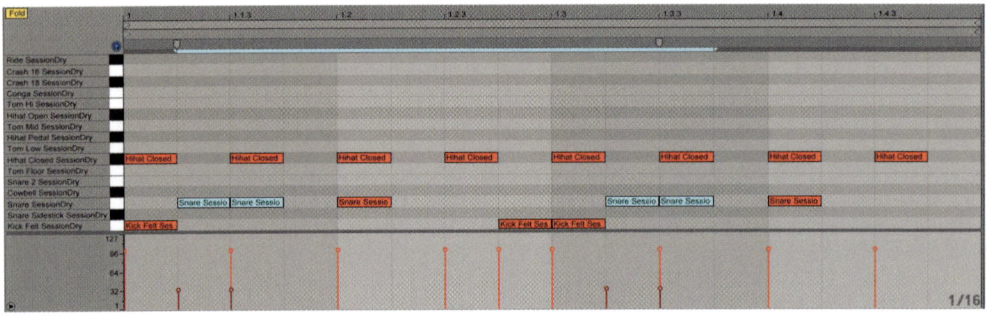

The additional low-velocity snare notes on the second and third sixteenths of beats one and three help to propel the musical time forward.

Another nice use of ghost notes is for adding very quick gestures that lead into or "anticipate" important structural points in the groove, such as the downbeat. Here's an example:

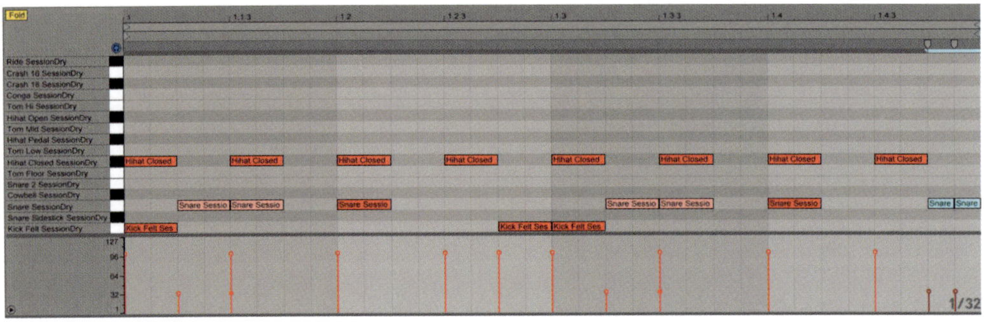

The blue notes are the thirty-second notes that drive towards the downbeat and might be heard in combination with the downbeat's kick drum hit as a single musical gesture.

To exaggerate this effect even more, some drummers will even play these thirty-second notes quite a bit behind the beat (see Programming Beats 1: On Looseness (page 166)):

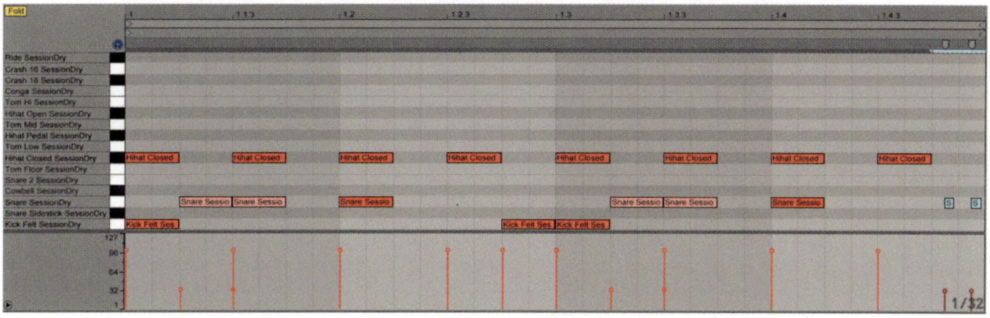

Note that when programming ghost notes in a DAW, the actual musical result is entirely dependent on how velocity-sensitive the instrument is that's being triggered. If you're using a drum machine for example, there may be no velocity variation at all, in which case adding ghost notes will simply create a different pattern. Ghost notes are usually most effective if you're triggering multisampled acoustic drums, in which there are actually low-velocity samples that will respond the way a real drum would respond. But of course, these techniques can also work with entirely electronic sounds as well. And although drummers usually play their ghost notes on the snare, you can also experiment with moving your ghost notes to an entirely different instrument.

Programming Beats 4: Top, Bottom, Left, Right

Problem:

From listening to a lot of music, you have a general understanding of how to program beats that sound similar to those in the music that inspires you. But you don't really have a sense of how the various drums in a drum kit relate to each other or the way human drummers think when they sit down at the drums and play. As a result, you're concerned that your programmed beats are either too mechanical sounding or are simply the result of your own interpretation and guesswork about what you hear in other music.

Even if you have no intention of writing "human"-sounding drum parts, it can be helpful to understand some of the physical implications of playing a real drum kit. Here are some ways that drummers approach their instrument.

Solution:

At a philosophical level, a drum kit can be thought of as divided into top and bottom halves. The top half includes all of the cymbals: the hi-hat, ride, crashes, and possibly more esoteric cymbals like splashes, Chinese cymbals, gongs, etc. These are the "top" half for two reasons: They're both physically higher than the drums, and they also occupy a higher range in the frequency spectrum. In contrast, the bottom half is the drums themselves: the kick, snare, and toms. (The snare is a special case and can be thought of as somewhere in between the top and the bottom in frequency. But for our purposes, let's consider it part of the bottom group).

Drummers tend to unconsciously approach beat making from either the "top down" or the "bottom up," depending primarily on genre. Jazz drumming beats, for example, are generally built from the top down, with the ride cymbal pattern being the most important element, followed by the hi-hat (played by the foot). In this context, the kick and snare drum serve to accent or interrupt the pattern which is established by the cymbals. A typical jazz drumming pattern might look like this:

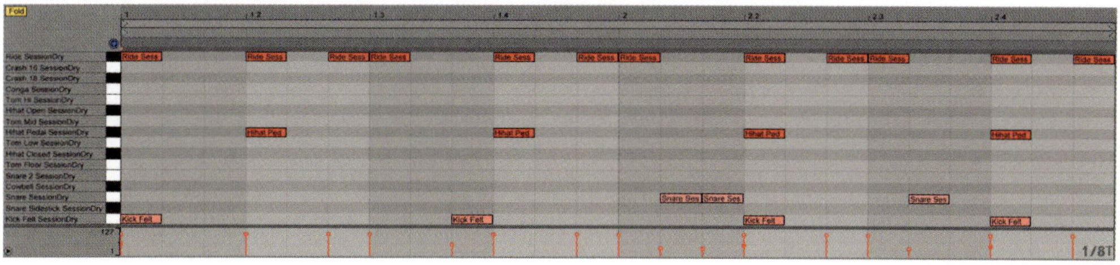

In contrast, rock, pop, or R&B drumming beats are built from the bottom up, with the interplay between the kick and the snare comprising the most important layer and the hi-hat or ride cymbal patterns serving as a secondary element. A typical rock drumming pattern might look like this:

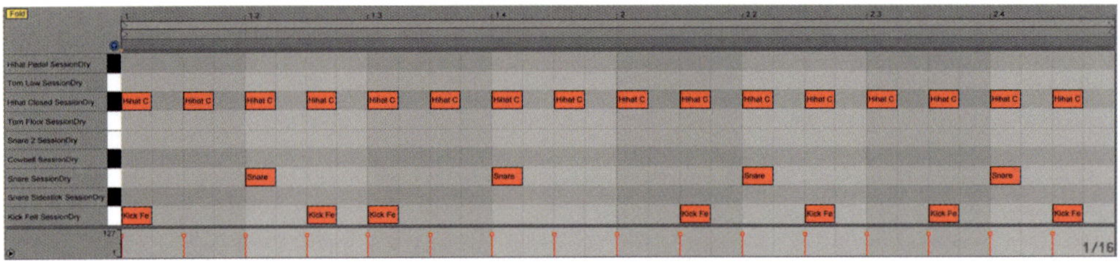

Note that in both jazz and rock beats, the cymbals generally play simple, repeating patterns, while the kick and snare play gestures that are more asymmetrical. But in jazz, those simple cymbal patterns are fundamental signifiers of the genre. In rock, the cymbal patterns are secondary in importance, while the asymmetrical kick and snare gestures are what define the music.

An awareness of these drumming concepts might give you some things to think about when writing your own electronic drum parts. Are you thinking from the top (cymbals) down, or from the bottom (kick and snare) up? Is the genre you're working in defined by repeating patterns (such as the steady four-on-the-floor kick drum of house and techno) or by asymmetrical gestures (such as the snare rolls used for buildups in trance)?

In addition to the top/bottom dichotomy, drummers also must make decisions along the left/right axis when determining how a particular pattern is divided between the left and right hands. On a drum kit, some of this is determined by the physical location of the instruments.

But for an instrument like a hi-hat that can be reached by either hand, there is often a subtle difference in sound depending on how the pattern is played. For example, consider the following beat:

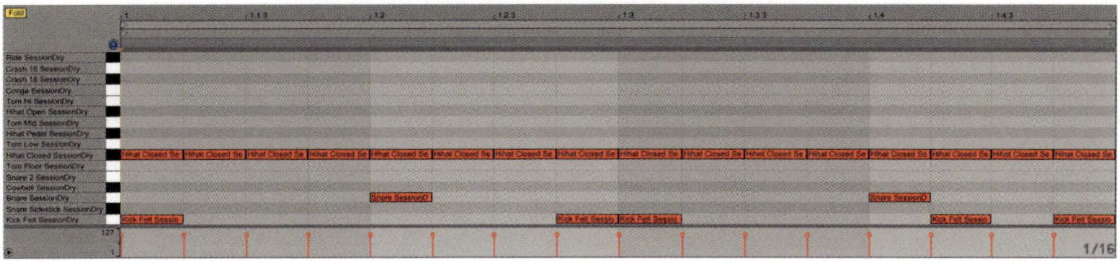

At slow-to-moderate tempos, most drummers would probably play the hi-hat part with one hand, leaving the other free for the snare drum. But once the tempo becomes too fast, it's no longer possible to play a continuous stream of sixteenth notes with one hand. At this point, many drummers would switch to playing the hi-hat with alternating sticking, each stroke with the opposite hand. But this requires some compromises: Beats two and four require both hands to be playing together, so the player must either move one hand very quickly between the snare and hi-hat or play at least two consecutive hi-hat notes with the same hand. In both cases, there will likely be a slightly different resulting sound. Even the subtle physical differences between two drumsticks can result in a different sound versus when a pattern is played with a single hand.

Of course, none of these physical restrictions apply to the electronic domain by default. There's no inherent physical speed limit and no need for any notion of "alternating stickings." At any tempo, consecutive notes can sound completely identical if that's your intent. But if you'd like to apply some of the sonic characteristics that come about as a result of these human restrictions, you can do so manually. For example, you could try creating a very small change in velocity for every other note in a repeating pattern. Or with a bit more work, you could actually use a slightly different sound for every other note. Some software samplers have a feature called "round robin" that automatically plays a different sample with each key press.

Thinking like a drummer can be a useful exercise when writing beats for any genre—even ones that have no overt relationship to acoustic music at all.

Bass Lines and Kick Drums as a Single Composite

Problem:

You've learned all of the engineering tricks and technical solutions for a clean, well-defined low end. You use sidechain compression on your bass lines and EQ to remove unnecessary low-frequency information on every track besides kick and bass. But somehow, you're just not able to achieve the same clarity and definition in the bass as the tracks you admire. You know you're doing everything right technically, but things still sound muddy.

One of the most commonly discussed areas in music production is how to deal with issues in the low end. The solutions provided are almost always on the *production* side:

> Use EQ to create space for the bass in the kick drum's track, and vice versa.

> Use EQ on every other track to remove low end, which makes room for both kick and bass while reducing overall signal level.

> Use sidechain compression to automatically reduce the gain of the bass when the kick is sounding.

But what's discussed much less frequently is how to solve these problems on the *musical* side. Here are some compositional ideas for improving the clarity of low end.

Solution:

Rather than thinking of your kick and bass as two separate musical lines, try to think of them as a single composite monophonic line. In this scenario, you not only can't have more than one bass note playing simultaneously, you also can't play a bass note at the same time as the kick. This requires you to make compositional decisions; how can you create a bass line that fits between the notes in your kick drum pattern (and vice versa)?

In some genres (such as trance and some flavors of commercial EDM), bass notes are commonly placed only on offbeats, while the kick drum notes occur on every downbeat. This is a simple way of creating a single composite line and is a defining characteristic of music in these genres.

The image below is an example of a characteristic trance bass line (the red notes), with the kick drum pattern added below (the blue notes).

Other genres have less strict "rules" governing the relationship between kick and bass drum. In techno or house, for example, the kick drum is still often placed on every beat, but bass lines might be much more rhythmically intricate. Here's an example of a more detailed bass line (again shown alongside the kick drum notes) that still adheres to the notion of the kick and bass elements forming a monophonic composite.

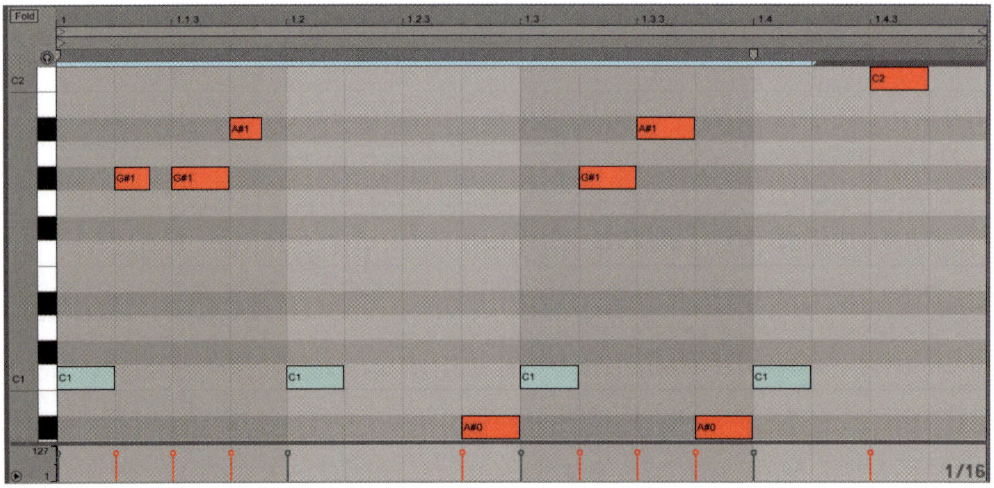

Notice that, in both of the above examples, neither the beginnings *nor the endings* of the bass line notes ever overlap the kick drum notes (or each other). Provided your kick and bass sounds are short, these patterns should create a very clean, truly monophonic composite, which should help maintain sonic clarity in the low end. But the duration of sounds can have a big impact on the effectiveness of this type of writing, and what you see in your patterns may not represent the reality of what you hear. For example, 808-style kick drums often sustain for a long time, so even though you've programmed short notes in your MIDI editor, the resultant sounds may still overlap, causing low-end interference. On the other hand, there may be some situations in which zero overlap can sound clipped and unnatural, and sustained notes make more musical sense. In these cases, you can still achieve a lot of the benefits of this composite technique by at least making sure that the attacks of the notes never overlap. Here's an example of long, sustained bass notes but with the note onsets themselves still carefully composed to stay out of the way of the kick drum line.

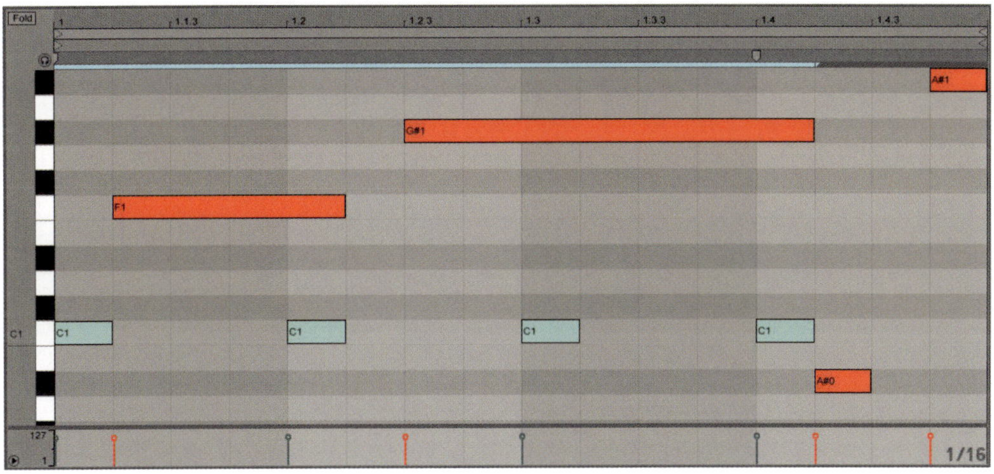

If, after applying these techniques, you find that you're still having problems with low-end clarity, you can always go back and apply the production tips mentioned previously. And since you've already composed your way out of the most severe issues, techniques like sidechain compression and low-cut EQing may now have a much more pronounced effect.

~ Note: In the examples mentioned here, the kick drum pattern has been added purely as a visual reference. But it might make sense for you to actually do this in your own music by copying the notes of the kick drum clips, pasting them into your bass clips, and then deactivating or muting them so they don't make sound. This creates a clear visual relationship between the bass and kick lines, making it easier to write as if they were a single line.

Drums to Pitches and Vice Versa

Problem:

Sometimes you have great ideas for drum patterns but aren't able to find melodies or harmonies that fit. Other times, you have the opposite problem: You come up with great pitched ideas but can't write drum parts that work with them.

It's common to write bits and pieces of songs in no particular order. In fact, this kind of Goal-less Exploration (page 78) can be a great way to spend creative time without the pressure of needing to finish a song. And ideas created in this way can often be saved as Scraps and Sketches (page 94) to be revisited later. But sometimes, you really do want to finish the song but only seem to be able to compose one type of part.

Solution:

One of the greatest benefits of working with MIDI is that the notes of a musical idea are a completely different type of data than the sounds triggered by those notes. This means that the notes can be repurposed to play an entirely different sound. It's common to create a bass line, for example, and then try it out through a number of different bass sounds before finding the one that fits the best. What's less common, however, is using the MIDI notes created for one instrument to trigger a completely different category of instrument. And doing this can yield some really interesting results.

For example, let's take this drum pattern, which might be appropriate for house or related genres:

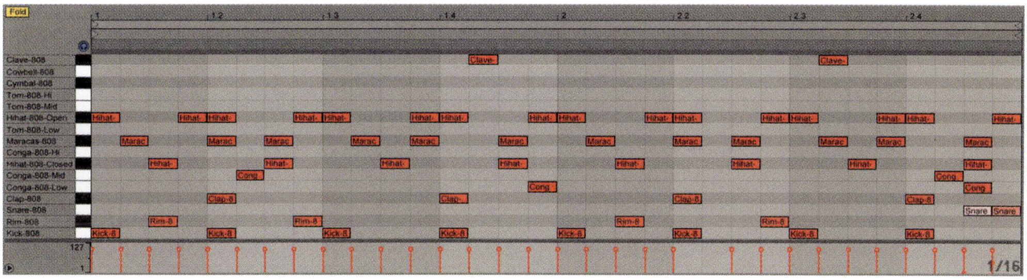

By simply copying this clip to a track containing a pitched instrument, we end up with this:

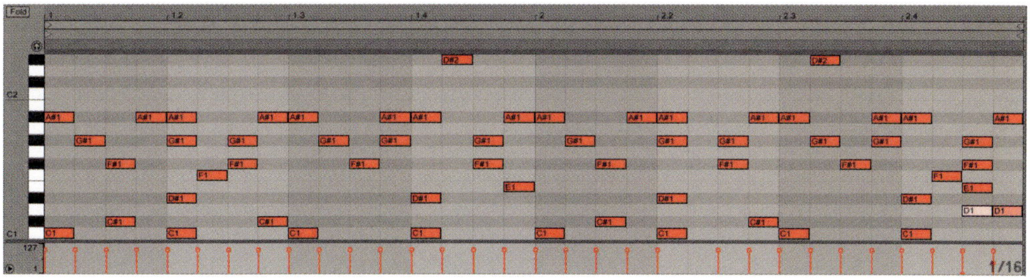

The resulting notes are "mapped" from the notes that triggered the appropriate drum sounds in the original clip. These sound a bit strange when played as they are. They're quite low in pitch, so the resulting chords sound somewhat thick and muddy. Also, the actual pitches aren't particularly harmonious (although this might be exactly what you want, depending on the music you're making). But the pattern is rhythmically and structurally interesting, and there are a number of things we can do to make the notes work better (see Creating Variation 3: Note Transformations (page 134)), including simply transposing the whole pattern to a higher octave. Another way to get the notes to work together better is to selectively transpose some of them—either manually, by dragging them to new pitches, or automatically, through the use of some sort of scale-correcting MIDI effect (if your DAW has one). Now, in just a few steps, you've created a melodic or harmonic pattern that's musically related to the drum pattern (because it's rhythmically identical) and which might be useful as an idea in your song.

Of course, you can also follow this process in the other direction. If you have an interesting melodic or harmonic part, try copying the clip to a track containing drums. You'll probably end up with a lot of strange drum choices, but you'll likely get an interesting rhythmic pattern. By transposing the notes so that they play more appropriate drums, you might end up with an interesting drum part that you never would have written otherwise.

Some DAWs and plug-ins allow you to analyze recordings of audio and extract the pitch and rhythmic information into new MIDI clips. While this functionality is normally used to extract specific types of audio recordings into similar types of MIDI recordings, you might get interesting results if you use the "wrong" algorithm when converting. For example, if you're converting a piece of polyphonic audio, try telling your conversion utility that the material actually consists of drums instead. The tool will then try to figure out the pitches implied by the drums, which will likely result in harmonies that are completely unexpected (but which might be musically interesting).

What's exciting about these possibilities isn't just that you can create lots of new ideas from a small amount of source material, but also that the resulting ideas will be musically connected to their sources. While it might be boring to simply play the same rhythmic idea in the drums and a pitched part simultaneously, having real musical connections between the two allows you to alter one or the other in a way that makes the new part unique but still identifiable as a "descendant" of the original part.

Tuning Everything

Problem:

You're happy with all of the parts of your song, and the arrangement feels right. You're happy with all of the sounds as well—but only when you listen to them in isolation. When you listen to everything together, the energy and power that you hear in the individual parts seems to get blurred or lost. You've done all of the EQing and production tricks to make space for the various parts in the mix, but it still isn't working.

Sometimes there are musical factors, rather than production ones, that greatly affect whether or not a mix "gels" into a single, cohesive sound. One of the most important—and most overlooked—musical considerations is tuning. Here are some tips for ensuring that all of the elements in your mix are in tune with each other.

Solution:

Producers are generally pretty careful about making sure that the overtly pitched elements in their tracks are in tune with each other. Except in some experimental genres where unusual tuning relationships are a fundamental part of the musical concept, things like bass lines, harmony parts, and melodic elements sound terrible when their tunings don't match. But producers are often less careful when it comes to tuning elements like drums, which typically have a less definite pitch. In genres that use acoustic drums, this isn't usually an issue; acoustic drums are generally heard as unpitched. (The exception is toms, which often are tuned both to each other and to the key of the song.) But in electronic music, drum sounds are often generated via synthesis; kick drums are often made from pure sine waves, for example. And in these cases, drums may actually have a clearly audible pitch that should usually be tuned to the other instruments in the song.

As mentioned earlier, electronic kick drums are the most obvious candidates for tuning, especially if they're made from sustained sine waves. And as with acoustic toms, electronic toms are also often clearly pitched. If you're using toms in your song, you probably don't want them all at the same pitch, so it might make sense to tune them in intervals that spell out the song's root chord. For example, a song in C minor might work well with the kick tuned to a C and toms tuned to an E♭ and a G.

But even other percussion sounds with less obvious pitches can often still be tuned. Wooden and metallic sounds, such as sampled or synthesized woodblocks and cowbells, often have a clear pitch. And even cymbals, snares, claps, and other "noisy" sounds can sometimes be tunable. You may not hear a pitch when listening to these sounds for the first time, but over the course of a whole song, certain frequencies within almost any sound will start to come to the forefront and will likely be perceived as the pitch of that sound.

In situations where you're working with noisy sounds, the pitch may be hard to identify, but you may still hear that it's wrong. A spectrum analyzer, in conjunction with an EQ, can be really helpful in these cases. You can use the spectrum analyzer to find the frequencies that are louder than the average noise level, and then use EQ to either emphasize those frequencies (if they happen to be in tune) or attenuate them (if they're out of tune with respect to the harmonic and melodic parts).

If you've committed to tuning your drums to the key of your song, but you're writing a song that changes keys part way through, you'll need to make decisions about whether to retune the drums as well. In some cases, simply retuning the kick and toms might be enough. But you'll need to carefully listen and think about how the drums work in relation to the other parts after the key change and adjust as necessary. In many cases, it may sound odd for the drums to suddenly be repitched. Ideally, drum tuning shouldn't be noticeable to most listeners; drums that are in tune with the other instruments shouldn't sound pitched. Instead, they should just make the whole song feel more like a single, cohesive entity.

Silence and Noise

Problem:

You understand that the fundamental components of music are sound, harmony, melody, rhythm, and form. But you're sure there's something else that's happening in the music that inspires you, and you can't quite find it in your own music.

It's common to think that the "music" is what you directly hear—the notes that play instruments that fill up what would otherwise be empty space. But a more interesting approach is to recognize and take advantage of the fact that silence and incidental noise can be made into fundamental parts of the musical texture. They can be as much a component of the sound of your music as a bass line.

Here are some ways that you can start to use silence and noise in your own music.

Solution:

Listen to other music and think about what's happening in the spaces between the notes. Is there ever actually complete silence? In most music, you'll probably find that at any given moment, there's always at least something you can hear. Even in sparse textures, there's usually a bit of reverb, delay, or other ambience that fills the gaps between notes. You can usually achieve this texture pretty easily by adding subtle spatial effects to certain elements.

But in some music, the space between the notes is truly silent. Listen, for example, to music by artists such as Atom™. Here, reverb is used sparingly, and each musical gesture seems to enter and exit against a backdrop of empty space. The result is an overall texture that's extremely clean, surgically precise, and very "digital." To make music that evokes this feeling, you'll need to be very careful with spatial effects, as well as with the placement and duration of your sounds. Long sustained chords might not make sense in this context, nor will sounds with slow attacks or releases. It might help to think of everything as a short, percussive element.

At the other end of the spectrum, some music has no silence at all, with every gap between notes filled with some kind of ambience or noise that is so present that it's as important to the texture as the "intentional" sounds. Dub techno, as exemplified by artists such as Rhythm & Sound, is largely defined by this approach to space. Although the instrumental layers are quite sparse, there is a constant layer of noise that suggests the use of mysterious, ancient, broken equipment. This type of ambience might seem hard to achieve in modern, ultra-clean DAW environments, but here are some ways to create it:

> Record the sound of an open microphone in a quiet room (or even just a channel on your audio interface with nothing connected) and then dramatically boost the level of the recording. The inherent noise of mics, preamps, and audio interfaces can take on a new character when boosted enough to be heard as an intentional element in a mix.

- Sample the sound of a turntable's needle in the "runout" groove at the end of a vinyl record.
- Field recordings of almost any source can take on the character of abstract noise, provided they're processed in the right ways. Try applying lots of reverb to urban, factory, or nature recordings.
- Certain plug-ins are designed specifically to create artificial noise, although these can sometimes sound quite consistent (and thus artificial) unless heavily processed.
- If your DAW has this functionality, try creating feedback loops by sending the output of a return track back into itself, (carefully) adjusting the send level, and then recording the output. You can create very interesting types of noise with this technique—especially when using effects on the return track.

Whether you're aiming to incorporate noise as a compositional element or are aiming for clinical, ultra-clean textures, it pays to think carefully about what's happening between the notes in your music and to make conscious decisions about how to make musical use of that space.

Sampling the Old-Fashioned Way

Problem:

You hear more and more music that uses samples in ways that sound like a deliberate under-leveraging of available technology. With characteristics such as "chipmunk vocals" and sampled breakbeats that sound like they're pitched up, a lot of contemporary garage, footwork, and related styles use a set of techniques that sound like they're taking advantage of the restrictions of vintage hardware. You'd like to be able to capture some of this nostalgic quality in your own music, but you can't seem to figure out how it's done using modern software tools.

One of the most important technical developments in sampling technology was the advent of *time-stretching*: adjusting the pitch of a sample independently of its tempo (and vice versa). Prior to time-stretching, pitch and tempo were inextricably linked; the only way to make a sample play at a higher pitch was to play it faster. Modern time-stretching technology is great for preserving the realism of retuned samples and allows for considerable flexibility in reusing rhythmic samples at a range of tempos. But some of the artifacts and quirks in the older approach imparted a lot of interesting musical character. Here's a technique for employing old-fashioned approaches to sampling in a creative way.

Solution:

In many modern DAWs, time-stretching is enabled by default for clips, under the assumption that this is the most flexible choice for most users in most musical situations. Although there is always a way to disable this functionality, either globally or on a per-clip basis, this usually just causes the clips to play back at their original tempo regardless of the tempo of the song. To really see what can happen when time-stretching is eliminated, try playing the samples from a software or hardware sampler instead of placing them along your song's timeline. Now, samples played at different pitches on the keyboard will also play at different tempos. This can yield particularly interesting results when working with samples that have their own inherent rhythm (such as breakbeats or whole musical phrases).

The track "Leavin" by DJ Rashad uses this technique to great effect. The main hook in the track uses a sample of a two-note pattern: a dotted eighth note followed by a sixteenth. The four-bar phrase consists of this sample triggered every half note. For the first two bars the sample is at its root pitch (E). In bar three, it's triggered three semitones higher (G). In bar four, it's triggered two semitones below the root (D). In a sequencer, the played pattern might look like this:

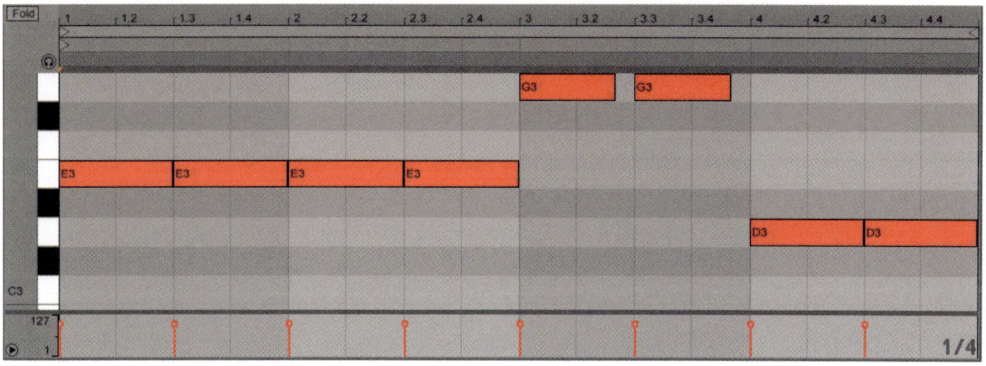

But because this is played using old-fashioned sampling technology, the transposed pitches play back the sample's two-note phrase at different speeds. What you hear is something closer to this:

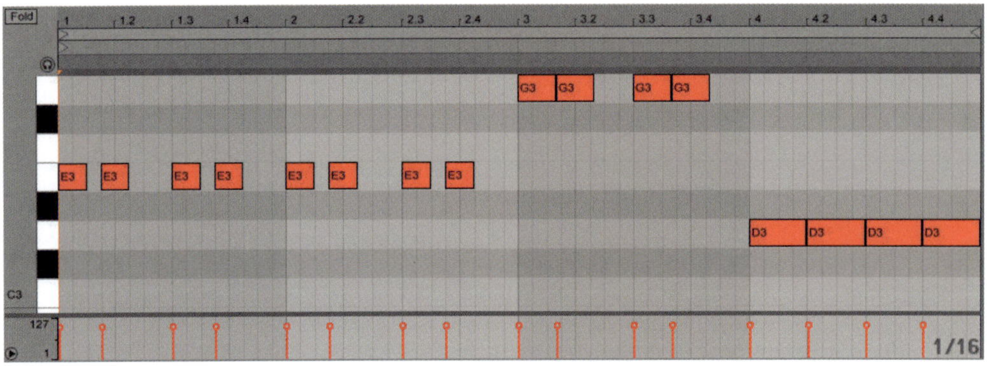

The first two bars play the dotted eighth/sixteenth pattern of the original sample. But the pattern in the next bar is transposed higher and thus plays faster—closer to the first two notes of a quarter note triplet. Finally the samples in the fourth bar play slower—closer to straight quarter notes.

If this sample were to have been triggered using a time-stretching sampler, there would be no rhythmic variation when transposing. The pitch would have changed, but the internal rhythm of the sample would have remained at a dotted eighth + sixteenth each time the sample was triggered. You'd hear something like this, which is much less interesting:

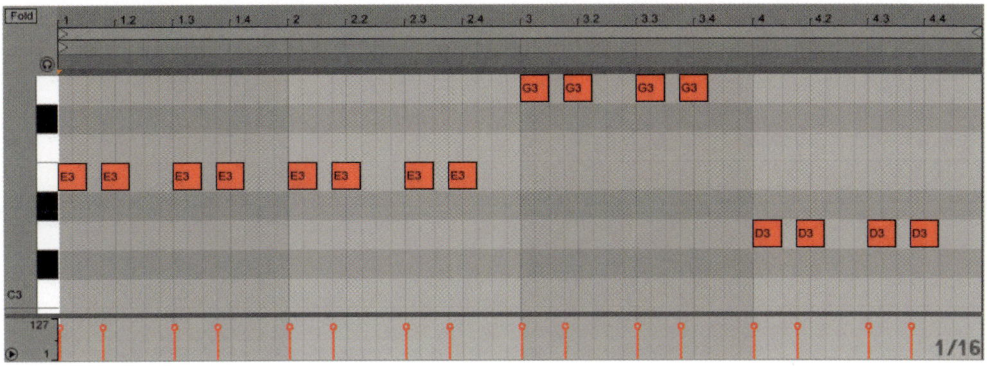

These examples may be easier to visualize in musical notation (but don't worry if you don't read music; these are simply notational representations of the three patterns shown previously).

What is played:

What you hear (as a result of using old-fashioned, non-time-stretched sampling):

What you would hear (if a time-stretching sampler were used):

By deliberately using an old-fashioned approach to sampling, DJ Rashad made use of the limitations in the technology to create a more interesting musical result than he could have achieved by using a more modern approach.

Creating Melodies 1: Contour

Problem:

When you listen to music that inspires you, the melodies are strong, memorable, and hummable. In contrast, your melodies feel weak, aimless, and wandering.

Writing a good melody is challenging. Here are some ideas for writing better melodies by thinking about their *contour*.

Solution:

The term contour is used to refer to the shape of a melody over time—whether the notes rise to higher pitches, fall to lower ones, remain at the same pitch, or some combination of these. Additionally, we use contour to discuss whether a melody moves by adjacent notes (known as *conjunct motion* or *motion by step*) or by larger intervals (known as *disjunct motion* or *motion by leap*).

A few general rules:

> Good melodies have a strong sense of balance between both aspects of contour: rise vs. fall and conjunct motion vs. disjunct motion. For example, if a melody rises for a while, it might make sense for it to then fall by roughly the same amount.

> If a melody has moved by step for a while, a good choice might be to then proceed by leap in the opposite direction. The converse also applies: Commonly, a melody that has moved by leap will then move by step in the opposite direction. One situation in which this might not be necessary is when a melody is simply an arpeggiation of a chord in the harmony. In these cases, the leaps between chord tones may sound "complete" even without stepwise resolution in the opposite direction.

> Good melodies often have a single peak note. That is, the highest pitch in the melody occurs only once. Furthermore, that peak note often (although certainly not always) occurs on a "strong" beat. (Assuming a 4/4 meter, the first and third beats are considered "strong" or "on" beats while the second and fourth are considered "weak" or "off" beats. As you subdivide beats into shorter note values such as eighths and sixteenths, the same rule applies. That is, the odd-numbered subdivisions are perceived as stronger than the even-numbered ones.)

Let's consider an example of a melody that (mostly) follows these rules:

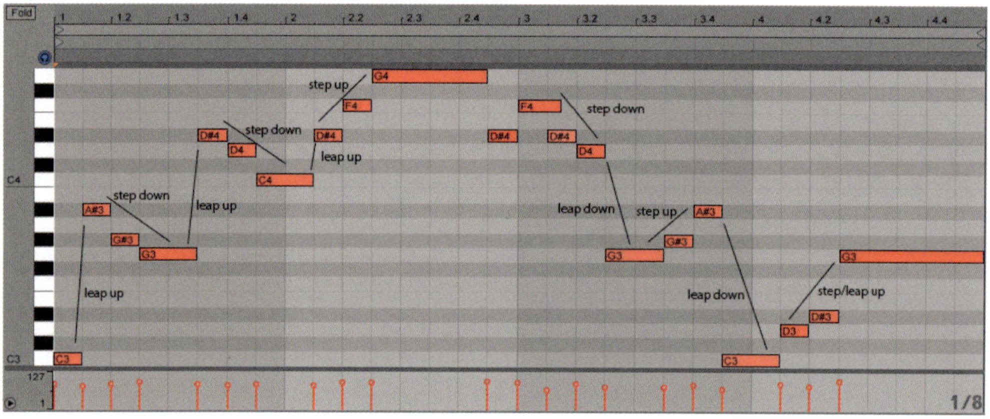

The melody opens with a large leap up, which is immediately followed by two notes that step down. This pattern is then repeated in the next passage. Following this, we "break" the rules briefly to reach the peak note: A leap up is followed by two steps up. The second half of the melody also strays a bit more from the rules. Bar 3 begins with a descending stepwise figure which is then followed by a leap in the same direction. Next, we step up, and then leap down. The final gesture breaks the rules once again: We step up and then continue upward by leap to the last note.

The general contour of the melody is a kind of arc: We start from the lowest note in the passage and climb gradually to the highest note at roughly the halfway point of the melody, before gradually descending again to cover roughly the same amount of space in the second half.

As you listen to other melodies with contour in mind, you'll find that most (including the one discussed earlier) don't follow these guidelines 100 percent of the time. But in general, you'll find that the contour of most good melodies maintains a balance between ascent and descent and stepwise and leapwise motion.

Creating Melodies 2: Using Motives

Problem:

When you listen to music that inspires you, the melodies are strong, memorable, and hummable. In contrast, your melodies feel weak, aimless, and wandering.

Writing a good melody is challenging. Here are some ideas for writing better melodies by using *motives*.

Solution:

Part of the reason writing melodies is so intimidating is that it's easy to imagine a melody as just a long string of notes without any internal logic. But melodies often have an inherent formal structure that is a sort of small-scale version of the formal structure used to construct a whole song. The smallest recognizable fragment of a melody is called a motive, and melodies are often constructed from just one or two motives. Motives are simple patterns that can be combined, repeated, and altered in various ways.

Here's an example of a melody from Daft Punk's "Doin' It Right" that's built from variations of just a single motive:

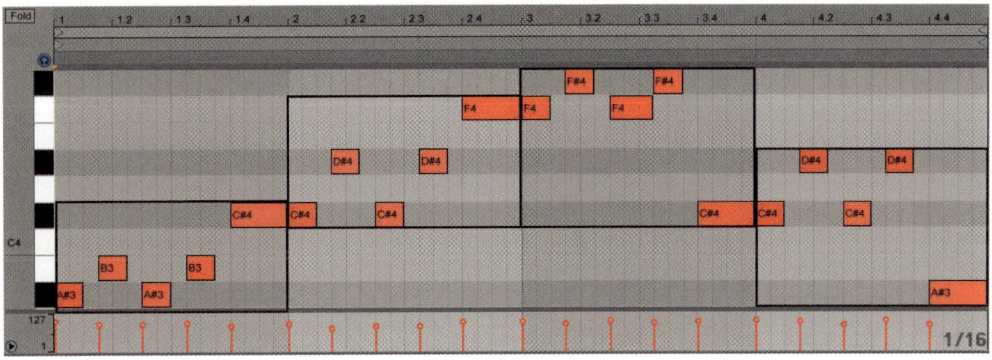

And here is the same example in musical notation:

In the MIDI example, the boxes outline each of the four sections of this melody, and each is a variation of the same five-note motive. In the first two bars, the first four notes are an ascending stepwise motive of two notes, repeated twice, while the fifth note is another stepwise ascent. In the second two bars, we again have the initial four notes built from the repeated two-note motive, but the fifth note is now a leap downward. The contour of the whole melody forms an arc, beginning and ending on the same note (see Creating Melodies 1: Contour (page 212)). In this example, a rich, usable melody is constructed simply by creating variations of a single five-note motive.

The melody in the chorus of Iggy Azalea's "Fancy" is a bit more complex but still uses variations of only two alternating motives. Here is the melody as MIDI notes:

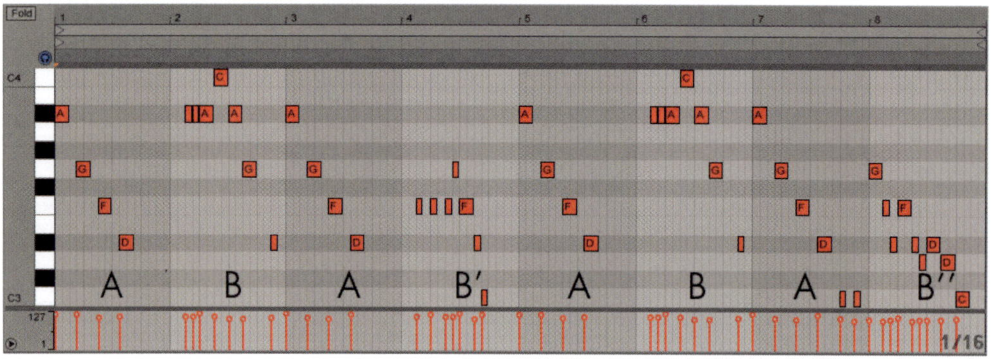

And here is the same example in musical notation:

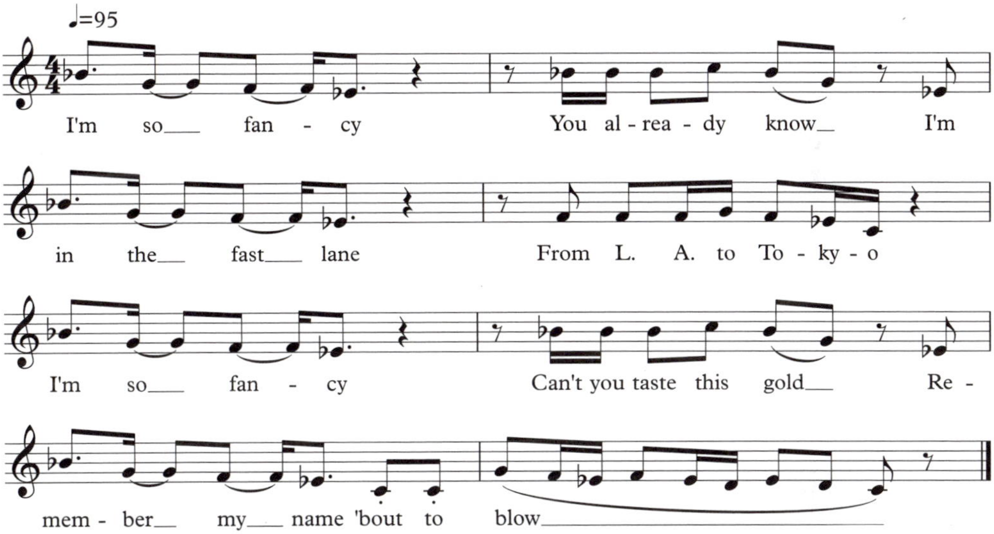

Each bar contains one of the two motives and these alternate every other bar. In the MIDI example, these are labeled as A and B. The A motives are repeated identically each time they occur, while the B motives are subject to variation. Bar four (labeled B') is essentially just a transposed version of bar two, with a slight rhythmic embellishment. And bar eight is just a more embellished version of bar four. Bar six is an identical repeat of bar two. The overall melody has a descending contour, as do each of the component motives.

As these examples show, there are many different ways to expand just one or two simple motives into a full melody through the use of variation. For some ideas about the kinds of variations you can use, see Creating Variations 3: Note Transformations (page 134). And identifying the motives in a melody can be a useful exercise when doing Active Listening (page 30).

Multiple Simultaneous Melodies

Problem:

In some music, you hear bass lines that are so detailed and interesting that they almost take on the quality of a melody. But when you try to do this in your own music, the parts collide and overlap in ways that just sound like a mess.

The combination of two or more intricate, independent, simultaneous melodies in a composition is called *counterpoint*. Here are some tips for how to use counterpoint effectively in your own work.

Solution:

Counterpoint is an old practice, and music with independent melodic lines has been written and studied for hundreds of years. There are very strict rules for writing "correct" counterpoint in ancient styles of music, and although music today is generally less strict in all ways, we can still take advantage of some of these rules if we want to write interesting counterpoint in contemporary music.

One example of counterpoint that you've probably come across is the *round*, a type of composition in which the same melody occurs in multiple parts but starting at different times. The children's songs *Row, Row, Row Your Boat* and *Frère Jacques* are examples of rounds.

Technically, any music with multiple monophonic parts (such as a melody and a bass line) could be considered counterpoint. But in most music, there is one clearly dominant melody while the bass line is much more rhythmically static or serves only to support the harmony (or both). We wouldn't normally refer to this type of music as counterpoint because the parts aren't given equal importance. True counterpoint (or at least good counterpoint) assumes that any of the parts involved in the counterpoint could function as a standalone melody even without the presence of the other parts.

An interesting example of counterpoint in electronic music is the Boards of Canada track "Roygbiv." The bass line is so intricate that, on first hearing, a listener might assume that it is really the track's melody. Only after the bass line has been repeated several times does the "real" melody finally enter. Here is a composite of the two parts:

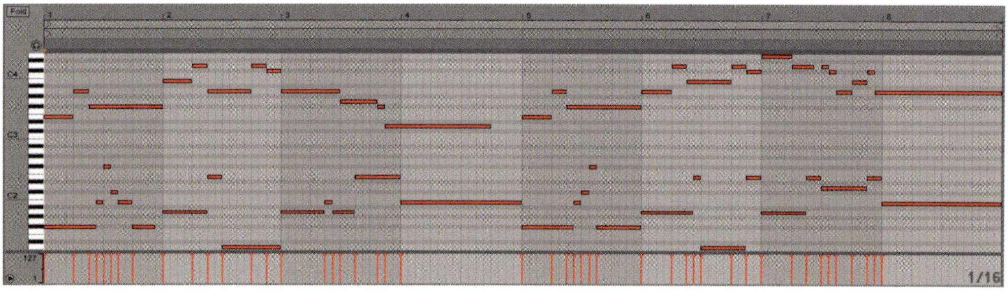

And here is the same composite in musical notation:

There are a few specific aspects to this counterpoint that make it so effective and that can serve as good guidelines for your own work:

Make sure that each part's rhythm is independent of the other parts. When parts move from note to note at the same time, our ears tend to hear the result as chords. The independence of the horizontal lines is lost, and we hear the vertical result instead. Successful counterpoint does result in good chords, but this is secondary to the melodic aspect. Notice how this is applied in the Boards of Canada example. With the exception of certain downbeats, each voice only moves to a new note when the other voice is sustaining.

Use contrary motion. As a general guideline, counterpoint works best when the voices mostly move in opposite directions; one voice moves up while the other moves down. This is known as *contrary motion*.

Be careful when crossing voices. In this example, each part stays within its own range of pitches, never crossing into the range of the other. This is straightforward here because the counterpoint is between a high melody and a low bass line. But in some cases, you might write two parts that could potentially cross each other. Brief voice crossings are generally not problematic, but if the parts are consistently winding around each other, they can lose their sense of independence. If you do want the voices to cross while still retaining their identity, try making the timbres of the parts highly distinct.

Not all music benefits from these techniques. In some cases, one melody—or even none—is enough. But if you're looking for ways to generate more complexity in your music, counterpoint might be a nice option.

Linear Rhythm in Melodies

Problem:

You can come up with the beginnings of a good melody, but you're looking for ways to generate more variations and complexity. In general, your melodic ideas don't have the depth or richness of those you admire.

Melodies are hard. Almost by definition, they are the most important and memorable aspect of a good piece of music. But coming up with one that's worth remembering feels almost as challenging as writing the entire rest of the song. Here is a technique you can try for generating more interest in your melodic writing.

Solution:

Hocket is a compositional technique in which the notes of a melodic line quickly alternate between two or more different instruments, such that no two instruments are playing at the same time. It is the melodic equivalent of linear drumming (see Programming Beats 2: Linear Drumming (page 172)) and can potentially turn bland melodies into interesting counterpoint. Hocket usually works best at fast tempos and when played by instruments with fast attacks and releases. It's a difficult technique for humans to play accurately but works really well for electronic music. As an example, let's begin with the simple loop below:

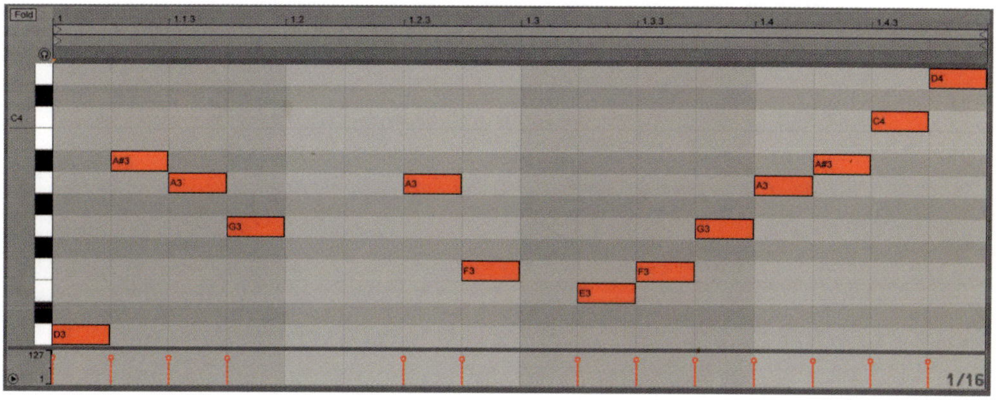

An easy recipe for turning this single voice into a hocketing pattern is as follows:

1. Duplicate the track, so that you have two identical copies of the pattern playing two separate (but so far, identical) instruments.
2. Modify the instrument in the new track so that it plays a different sound. This can be done by modifying or replacing the preset or even by replacing the instrument with a different one. As mentioned previously, try to find two instruments with similar volume contours. Short sounds with fast attacks work best.
3. Edit both patterns so that the melody is divided between them, such that no note is ever played by both instruments simultaneously. The way in which you divide the notes is entirely up to you, but really interesting hockets tend to alternate very quickly between the voices. The simplest example is probably literal alternation—the instruments trade off every other note. Here's how our original pattern might look if it was divided in this way:

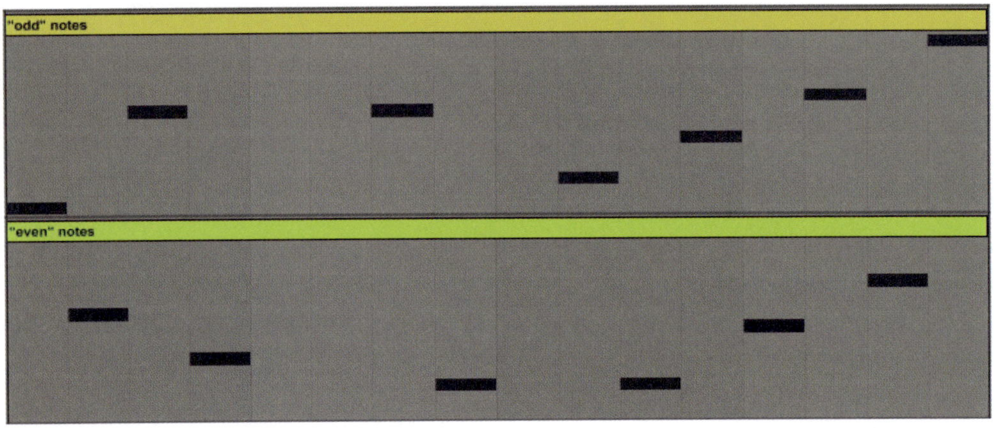

You could also alternate by larger note groupings, such as every quarter note:

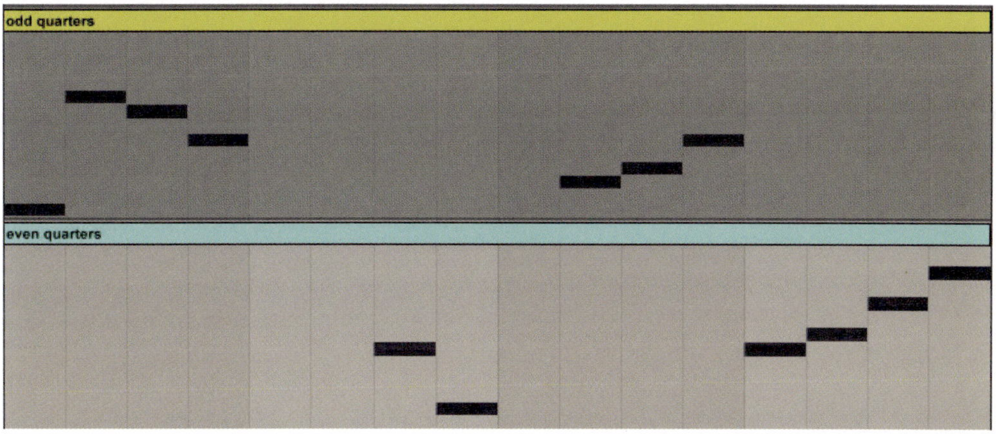

Or you could alternate by arbitrary time groupings, such as every third sixteenth (including rests):

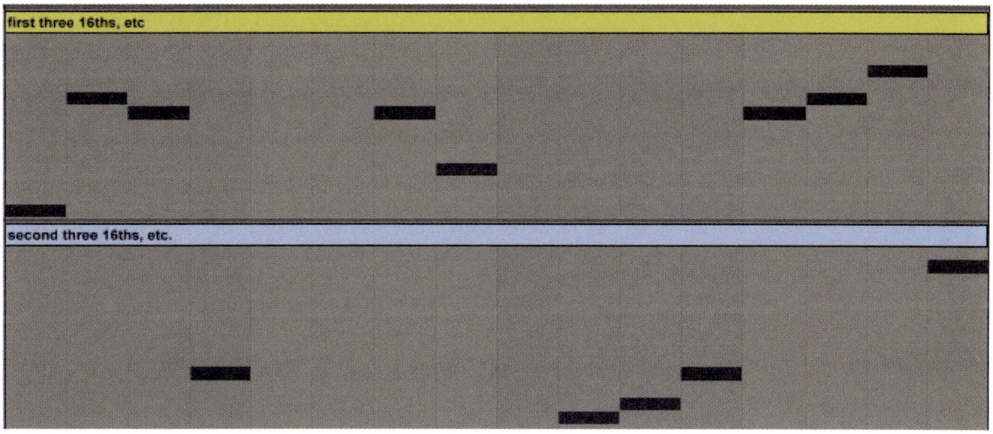

Notice that in the last example, the pattern doesn't divide evenly into groups of three sixteenths, so the final alternation is cut short in the bottom voice.

These examples illustrate some possibilities with a two-voice hocket, but even more possibilities become available when you use three or more voices. In an extreme example, each note could be played by a separate instrument. Hocket can give even the simplest melody a whole new life by subjecting it to a rapidly changing cascade of new timbres.

Sound-Color Melody

Problem:

You can write a strong, memorable melody. But especially at slow tempos, even if the notes and rhythms are right, you regularly get bored with the sound. You've tried programming parameter automation so that the timbre changes over time, but you still have the sense that the sound is too static.

Long, slow melodies are difficult to write effectively in electronic music. By default, synthesizer sounds don't tend to vary much from note to note, and even with careful use of modulation or automation to create a dynamic, changing sound, there can still be a sense that the timbre of the melody isn't "breathing" or is too artificial sounding. Here is a technique you can use to create more timbral variation, particularly in slow melodies.

Solution:

The German word *Klangfarbenmelodie* ("sound-color melody") refers to the distribution of a melody (or even a single pitch) between multiple instruments. This is a similar concept to hocket (see Linear Rhythm in Melodies (page 224)), although hocket generally refers to rapid, rhythmic transfer of melodic notes between voices at a fast tempo, while Klangfarbenmelodie is often slower and more subtle—one melodic voice gradually fading out as another fades in, for example.

Klangfarbenmelodie was originally developed as a technique for creating timbral variety in instrumental melodies, although it's perhaps even better suited for electronic music. For example, let's begin with the four-bar melody below:

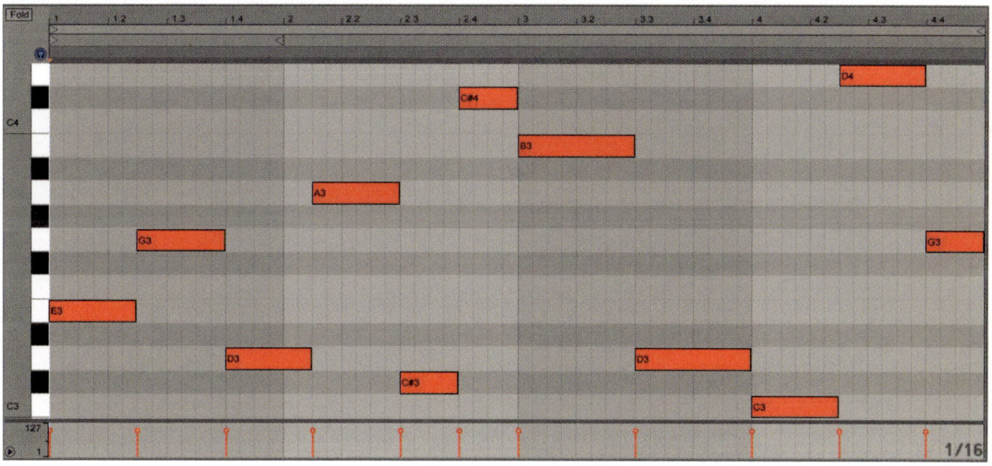

The conventional way to treat a melody like this would be to have it play on a track that triggered a software or hardware instrument. For a richer sound, perhaps multiple instruments could be layered or stacked. But another approach might be to split the higher-pitched notes from the lower-pitched ones, and route the two halves through different instruments. This particular melody is well-suited to this kind of treatment because of its "wedge-like" distribution of pitches. For example, we might arbitrarily decide that the high voice will play E3 and above, while the low voice plays everything below E3. Many DAWs allow for creating "split points" or "zones" within a single MIDI track, which take care of the MIDI routing automatically. In these cases, you can simply assign the split points as desired, load the two instruments onto the same track, and play the clip. If your DAW doesn't support this functionality, you could duplicate the track, modify or replace the second track's instrument, and then delete notes as necessary from each pattern so that the melody is divided between them in an interesting and musical way.

Unlike hocketing, where abrupt, jagged timbral changes are the intended musical result, the idea with Klangfarbenmelodie is to create a smooth, seamless exchange between voices. In the example melody discussed previously, another possibility might be to duplicate the track (or layer multiple instruments on a single track) but then use instruments that have "mirrored" volume envelopes. For example, one instrument might have a fast attack and a gradual decay, while the second instrument might have a slow attack. In this situation, the first instrument would supply the initial onset of the note, while the second instrument would fade in as the first faded away. Obviously, this requires carefully tuning the respective envelopes so that they make sense in the context of both the song's tempo and the duration of the notes in the pattern. But when configured properly, the result can be a slow timbral shift across the duration of each note.

These examples illustrate some possibilities with Klangfarbenmelodie across two voices, but even more possibilities become available when you use three or more voices.

The Rhythm of Lyrics

Problem:

Your vocal melodies feel wrong somehow, as if there's a "conflict" between the rhythm of the melody and the natural flow of the lyrics.

Writing vocal parts is a fundamentally more complicated problem than writing instrumental music because words and sentences have their own implicit rhythm that needs to be consciously considered. Here are some tips for understanding how to get your musical and textual rhythms to work together (or to counter each other, if that's your intention).

Solution:

Scansion is the study of a text's inherent rhythm and the marking of each syllable in the text as being either strongly or weakly *stressed*. We use these stress patterns naturally and unconsciously when speaking and, unless we're poets, probably never need to give them much thought outside of a musical context.

As an example: Let's pretend this sentence is a lyric in your song. (Note: Artistically, this is probably not a good idea.) When you read it out loud, you will naturally apply a stress or "accent" to some syllables, while others will be spoken more softly. We'll mark the strong syllables with a / and the weak ones with a *. (By convention, these stress markings are placed over the first vowel in the syllable.):

```
 /     * /     *   /  *    /  *  / *  /    *    /
Let's pretend this sentence is a lyric in your song.
```

Applying these markings can sometimes be subjective. For example, it could be argued that "is" is weakly stressed (although it is probably stressed slightly more than the "a" that follows it). But now that we have a general sense of the inherent stress patterns of the text, we can relate this directly to the inherent stress patterns of musical beats. A couple of general (but by no means universal) rules:

> (Assuming a 4/4 meter), the first and third beats are considered "strong" or "on" beats while the second and fourth are considered "weak" or "off" beats.

> As you subdivide beats into shorter note values such as eighths and sixteenths, the same rule applies. That is, the odd-numbered subdivisions are perceived as stronger than the even-numbered ones.

Placing strong syllables on strong beats and weak syllables on weak beats usually results in a fairly natural-sounding vocal melody, while doing the opposite can often sound forced or stilted. Additionally, you can reinforce these natural alignments further by making stressed syllables louder, higher in pitch, or longer in duration.

Here's an example of a possible melody for this lyric:

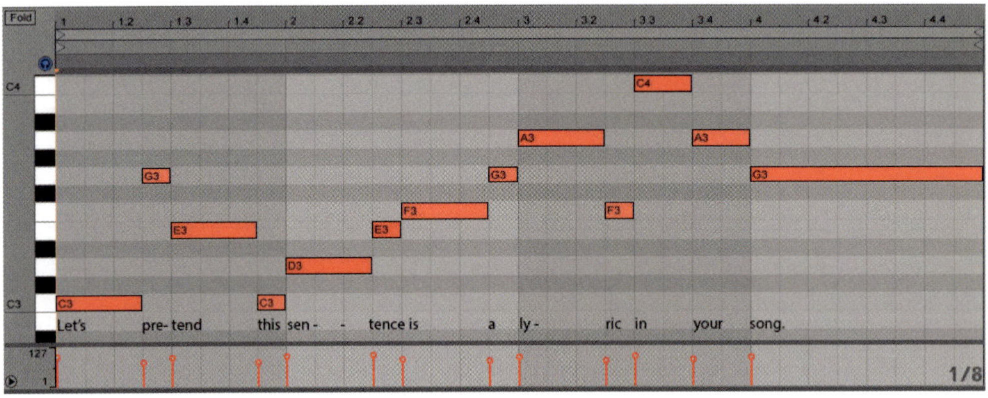

It's boring, but it "works" according to the scansion rules discussed earlier. Natural text accents occur on strong beat positions and are further emphasized by occurring on notes that last longer, while weakly stressed syllables occur on weak beats and have short durations.

To contrast, let's take a look at a possible melody that goes against the natural stresses of the lyric:

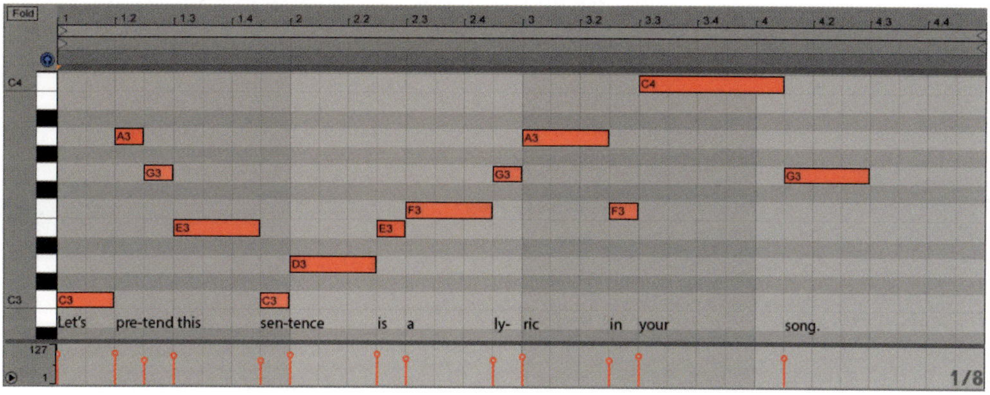

This is nearly identical to the first melody, but with an additional note added on beat two of the first bar in order to shift each syllable to the left. Now we're breaking all the rules. The weakly stressed syllables happen almost entirely on strong beats and are sustained for long note durations, while the strongly accented syllables are short and on weak beats. This would be both difficult to sing and uncomfortable to listen to.

Although good vocal melodies are often significantly more nuanced and rhythmically intricate than both of these examples, you'll find that most of the time, good melodies follow the natural patterns of stress in the lyrics. Of course, there are exceptions. A lot of contemporary hip-hop, for example, uses syncopation and unusual stress patterns to go against the rhythm of the text. And it's always possible to apply more than one syllable of text to a single sustained note or, conversely, sustain a single syllable of text across more than a single pitch. But these are conscious and genre-specific musical decisions. If you find that your own vocal writing tends to feel strained and unnatural, it might be because you're fighting against how the lyrics want to flow.

Creating Harmony 1: The Basics

Problem:

You don't know enough about how chords really "work" to understand how to get from one chord to another, and your attempts to create interesting chord progressions never match up to the music that inspires you.

Harmony is a big topic, and covering the full range of how chords work is beyond the scope of this book. But fortunately, the vast majority of what's commonly done with harmony in many types of music can be learned with just a bit of background and some basic terms. Here are some of the fundamentals.

Solution:

Most music is considered to be in a particular *key*. If we say that a song is "in C," this simply means that the note C sounds to most listeners like the most stable "home note" for the song. Key can be established in a few ways: either through Repetition and Insistence (page 272) or, more commonly, through the use of chord combinations that sound, to most listeners, like they want to *resolve* back to the home note. This sense of tension and resolution is the basis of most successful chord progressions.

If we continue to assume C is our key note (or *tonic*), we can then determine the other notes in the *scale* of the key. The two most common *qualities* of scales are *major* and *minor*. These terms refer to the particular pattern of note distances (or *intervals*) between the adjacent notes in the scale. The C Major scale contains the following notes (shown in both a MIDI piano roll and conventional notation):

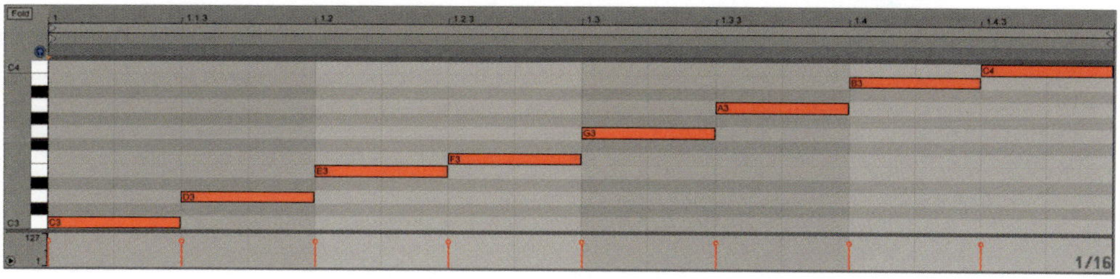

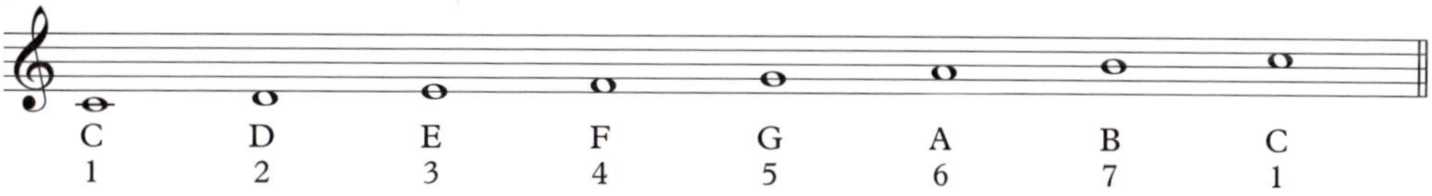

Although the examples in this chapter all use C as the tonic, you can easily transpose the examples in your DAW to try them out in any other key. Every major scale, regardless of starting note, contains seven notes (before repeating the first note again) and the same pattern of intervals between notes. That pattern is a particular combination of half steps (two immediately adjacent notes on the piano keyboard) and whole steps (notes that are two half steps apart): **Whole - Whole - Half - Whole - Whole - Whole - Half**:

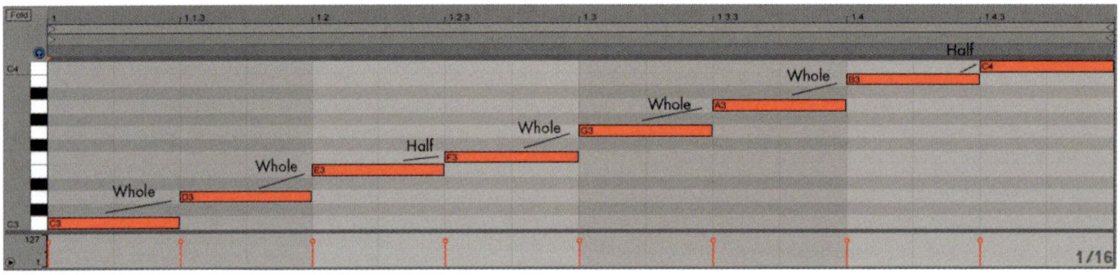

The minor scale contains a slightly different pattern of half and whole steps: **Whole - Half - Whole - Whole - Half - Whole - Whole**:

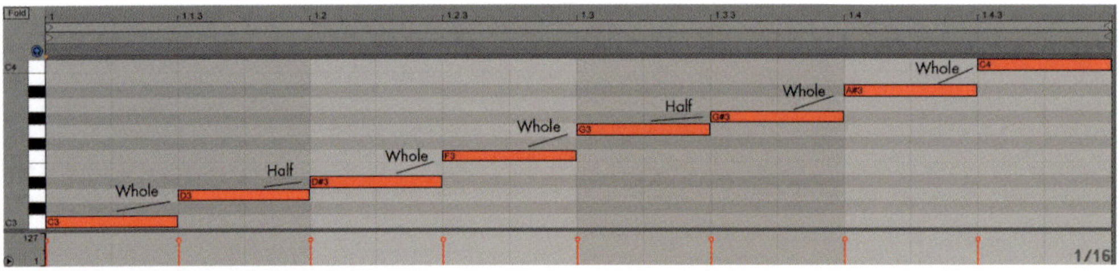

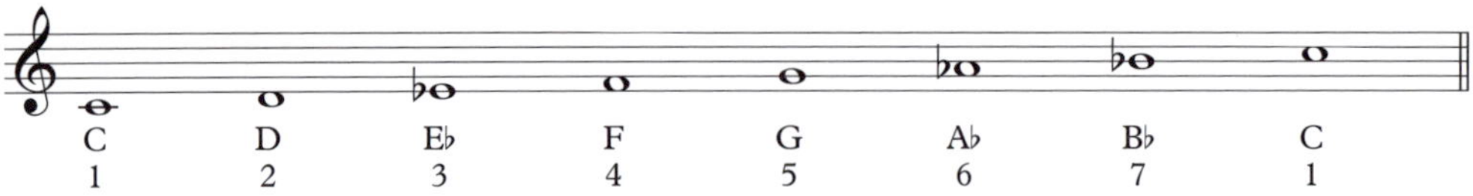

~ Note: Most DAWs use either only sharps or only flats in the piano roll. For our purposes here, consider D♯ = E♭, G♯ = A♭, and A♯ = B♭.

Now that we've established how major and minor scales are made, we can build chords on each of the notes in the scale. The most common chords are triads, which are built by adding the *third* and *fifth* notes above a starting note (or root). For example, in C Major, the triad built on C contains C (the root), E (the third note above C), and G (the fifth note above C). The triad built on A contains A (the root), C (the third note above A) and E (the fifth note above A). Here are the seven triads in C Major:

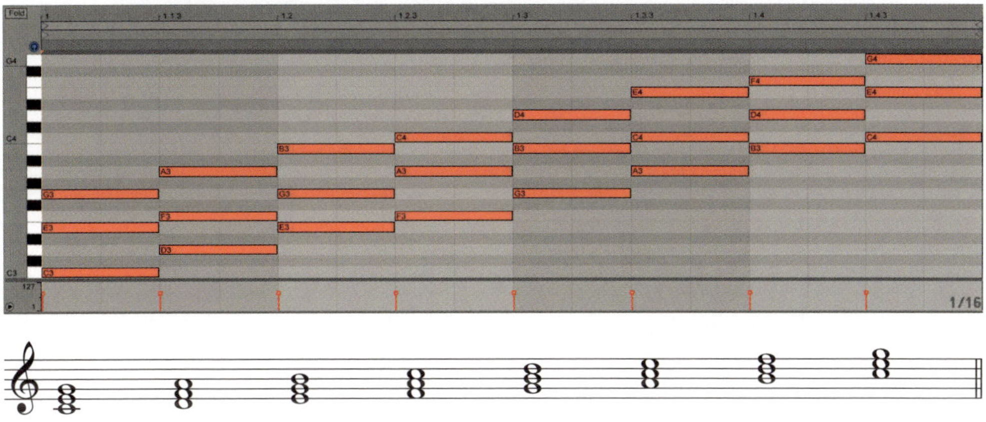

We referred earlier to the terms major and minor as being the *quality* of the key or scale. The triads in a particular key also have major or minor quality and, as with scales, this is determined by the interval distances between the notes. Major triads have four half steps between the root and the third note, while minor triads have only three. In both major and minor triads, there are seven half steps between the root and the fifth note. With this information, we can analyze and determine the quality of each triad in a particular key, simply by counting semitones.

Rather than using specific chord names (such as "C Major"), we can use Roman numerals for this type of chord analysis. This helps to emphasize an important aspect of this theory: Everything discussed here is completely transposable to any key, and all of the harmonic and scale relationships work exactly the same way regardless of which specific note is our tonic. By convention, major triads are labeled with capitalized Roman numerals, while minor triads are written with lower case Roman numerals. Here are the labels for the triads in the C Major scale:

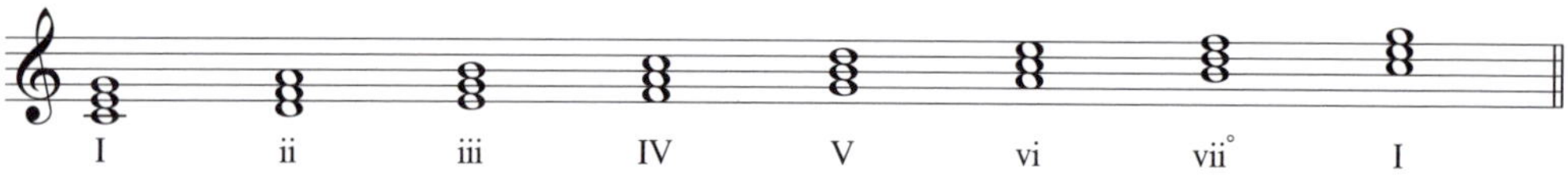

And the triads in the C minor scale:

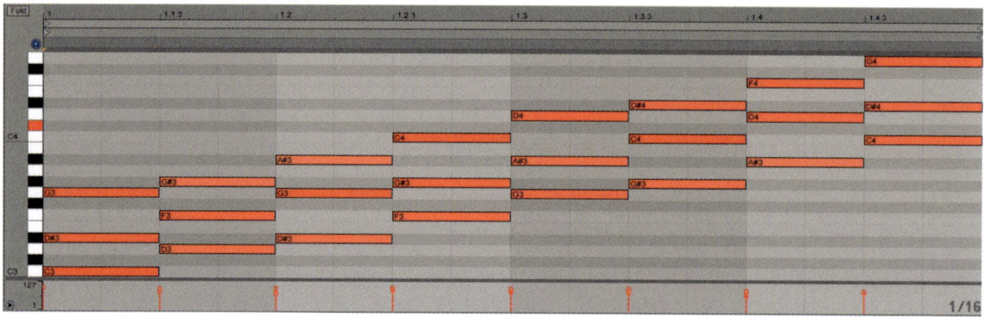

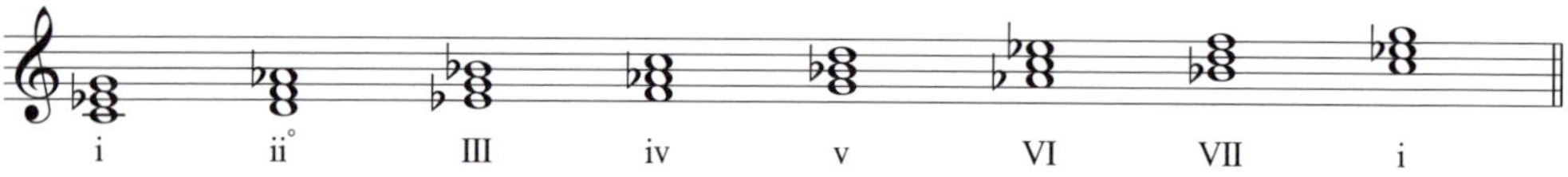

If you actually went through and measured the intervals in each of the triads above, you probably noticed that two of these chords don't fit into either the major or minor pattern. The seven chord in the major scale and the two chord in the minor scale are of a different quality, called *diminished*. Diminished triads, like minor triads, have three half steps between the root and the third note. But they have only six half steps between the root and the fifth note (as opposed to seven for the minor triad). Diminished triads are labeled with the superscript° after the Roman numeral.

It may sound surprising, but a huge amount of music, from the Classical period all the way to much contemporary pop and electronic music, uses *only* the seven chords that exist in a particular key (called the *diatonic* chords). And many songs use no more than two or three of these chords. But the choice and order of diatonic chords is what determines how the chord progression really sounds. What follows are a few general guidelines that can help you move from one chord to the next (Roman numerals refer to the major scale, but the patterns are similar for minor scales).

After a I chord, anything is possible; all chords within the key sound equally appropriate after the tonic chord. The V or vii° chords sound (to most listeners) like they "want" to resolve back to I (although V can sometimes lead to vi). The ii and IV chords have a tendency to lead towards the V or vii° (although IV also commonly leads back to I or to its "partner" ii). The vi chord leads to the ii or IV. And finally, the iii chord has a tendency to be followed by the vi. This series of chord resolutions can be summarized in this figure:

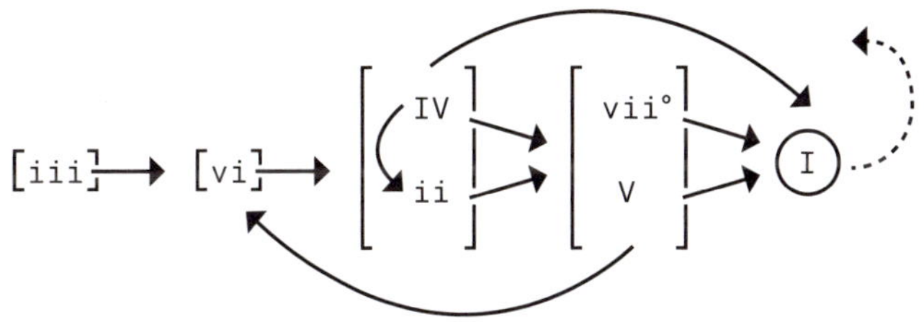

Using just these guidelines for diatonic triads, you have access to a huge number of usable chord progressions. For example, one of the most common progressions is I - V - vi - IV:

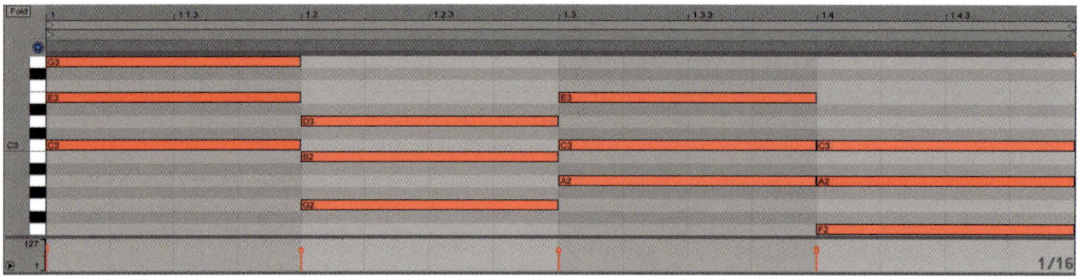

This is the progression in the verses of Imogen Heap's "Hide and Seek," the choruses of Adele's "Someone Like You," and many more. In fact, there are *countless* well-known songs that use this exact progression ("Four Chord Song" by Axis of Awesome is an enlightening mashup of 36 of them).

Chord progressions that follow these guidelines are said to be *functional* because each chord functions as a preparation for the next chord in the series. There is, of course, a much wider world of harmonic possibilities available beyond just using diatonic triads. But if you're interested in creating music that's within the realm of pop music, you can get quite far using only these seven chords.

~ Side note: A lot of the theory behind the construction of scales and triads may seem like arbitrary, rote memorization. Why did these particular combinations of whole and half steps come to define the scales that are commonly used? Why do certain chords have a feeling of "wanting" to move to other chords? Why do these scales and chords exist at all? Detailed answers are beyond the scope of this book but largely have to do with acoustics: The intervals of the major scale can be derived from fairly simple whole number frequency ratios that correspond to the overtone series. But perhaps even more importantly, much of this theory is *descriptive* rather than *prescriptive*: The theory was developed to help explain patterns in music that already existed, rather than to tell composers what they should or should not do in the future.

Creating Harmony 2: Beyond Triads

Problem:

From reading the previous chapter, you understand the fundamentals of triads and diatonic harmony, as well as how to use these tools to create usable chord progressions. But these chords lack the complexity and "color" that you hear in genres like jazz and even some house music. What else is possible?

Solution:

There are many types of chords besides diatonic triads. But the basic tools that we use to build those triads can also be used to create a much wider range of more complex chords. Here are a number of these chords, as well as some ideas about how to use them:

Seventh Chords

We know that triads are built by choosing a starting note (or root) and then adding the third and fifth notes above it. But we can extend this pattern by adding the seventh note above the root. The four-note chord that results is (conveniently) called a *seventh chord*. Here are the diatonic seventh chords in C Major (shown in both a MIDI piano roll and conventional notation):

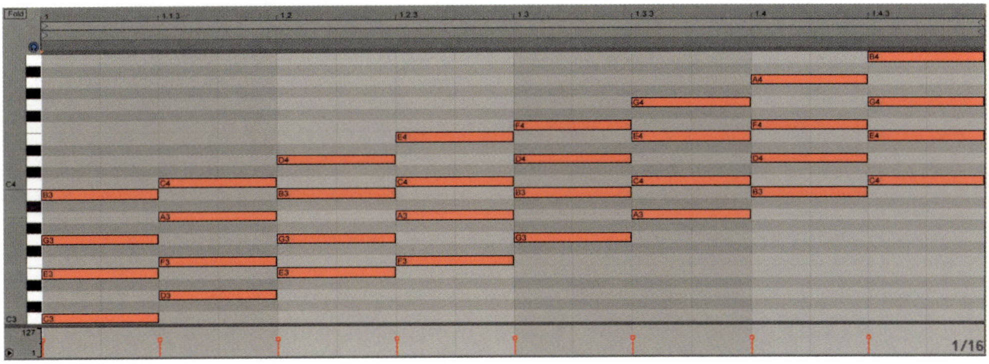

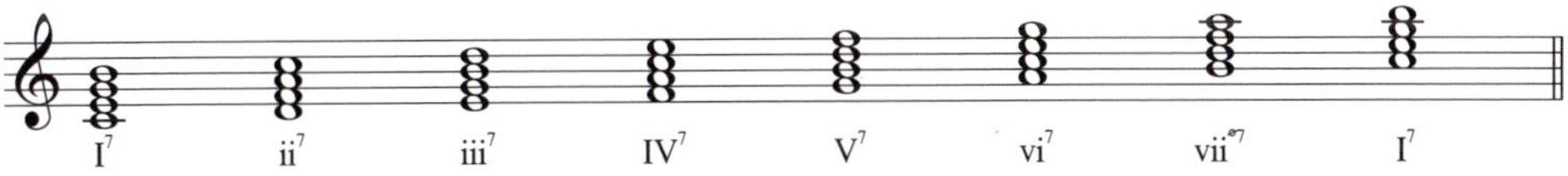

As with major, minor, and diminished triads, seventh chords also have a quality, although the situation becomes slightly more complex because the triad that serves as the basis of the chord does not necessarily have the same quality as the seventh itself. For example, the I and IV triads are both major, and so are the corresponding I^7 and IV^7 chords. This is because we define a major seventh as the interval distance of 11 half steps from the root to the seventh of the chord. But the V^7 is very interesting. The V triad is major, but the seventh is minor—ten half steps between the root and the seventh. This combination of a major triad with a minor seventh on top is called a *dominant* seventh chord and has a strong feeling of "wanting" to resolve to the I chord. The $vii^{\varnothing 7}$ is another interesting case. Here, the triad is diminished while the seventh is minor. This is known as a *half-diminished seventh chord*.

With the exception of the V^7, which is very commonly used to resolve back to I, seventh chords are used less frequently than triads in many genres. But they are the fundamental harmonic building blocks used in jazz and related genres. In fact, almost any "normal" functional chord progression (as explained in Creating Harmony 1: The Basics (page 238)) can be given a jazz flavor by replacing the triads with their corresponding diatonic seventh chords. Jazz often uses sevenths in "non-functional" ways as well, and jazz progressions often consist of chains of seventh chords that lead to one another primarily by smoothly connecting the individual voices within the chords and maintaining common tones whenever possible (rather than by use of predictable functionality). For more about how to make these kinds of progressions, see the chapter about Voice Leading and Inversions (page 260).

Further Extensions: 9ths, 11ths, and 13ths

We can extend this method of constructing triads and seventh chords even further simply by adding additional thirds to the top. With one additional note, we get 9th chords:

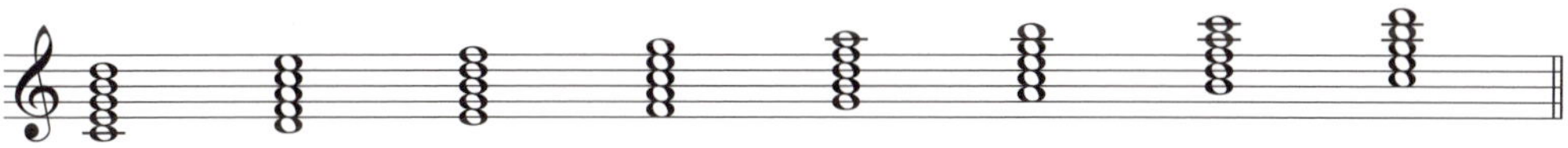

Add one more note to get 11th chords:

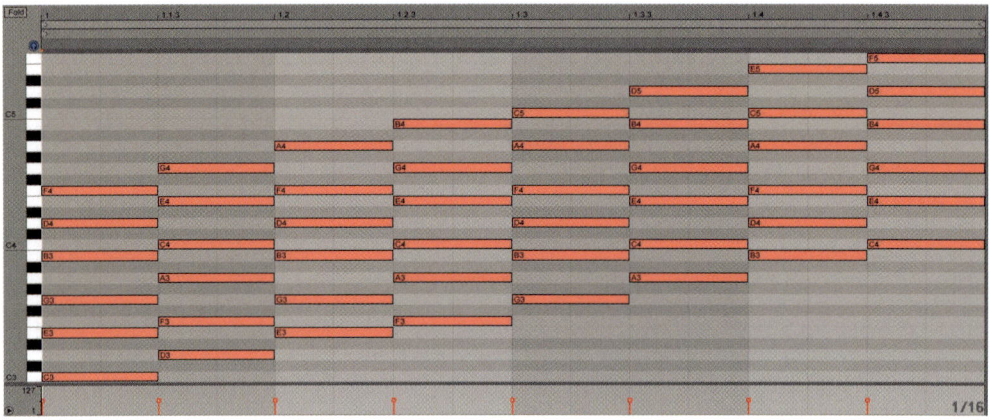

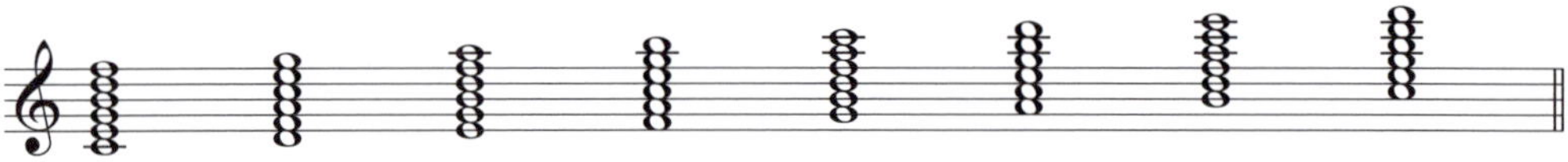

And finally, yet one more note creates 13th chords:

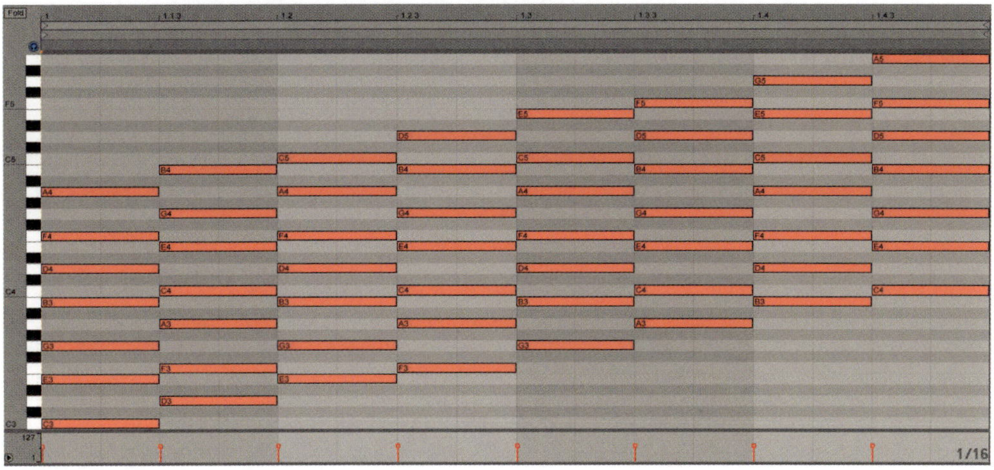

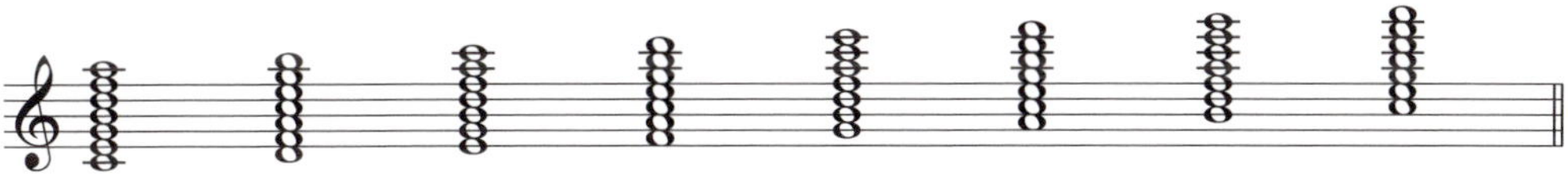

Note that I have left the Roman numeral analysis off of these chords. This is because the quality of these chords quickly becomes very complex, and also very ambiguous—in many cases, there is no single "correct" analysis for these large chords. It's also because these types of harmonies are not normally used in a functional context (with the exception of sometimes serving as replacements for conventional progressions of triads).

It is rare for keyboard players to play every note of these very large, dense harmonies. This is partly because it's difficult to quickly navigate the keyboard while playing seven-note chords, but also because the sound of these harmonies can be implied by playing only the most "important" notes in the structure—commonly the highest notes in the extension, plus maybe the third. The root is commonly omitted entirely, usually because it's filled in by the bass or another instrument. Although it is no problem to program a DAW to play every voice of huge chords like this, you may still want to avoid doing so because you can quickly overpower a mix with such enormous blocks of harmony.

Although diatonic 9th, 11th, and 13th chords are common in jazz, it is also common to alter one or more of the notes in the chords to create even more interesting colors. Altering a chord simply means replacing one or more of the notes with a note that is one half step away. Some common alterations include lowering the fifth note, as in this 9th chord:

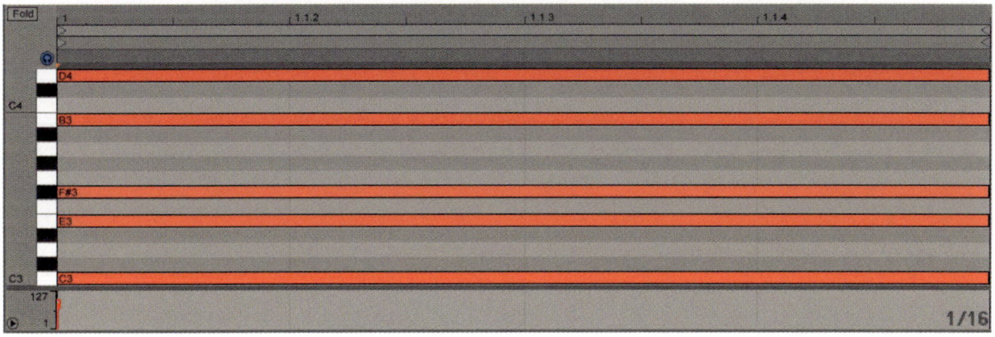

or raising the 11th.

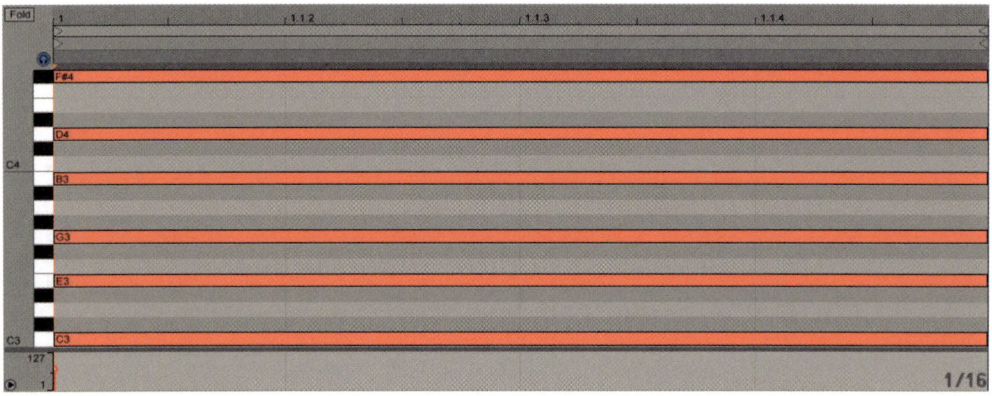

Notice that these chords are almost identical. In the first example, we've lowered the fifth of the chord, while in the second we've maintained the fifth while adding a raised 11th on top. But the lowered fifth (a G♭) and the raised 11th (an F♯) are the *same pitch*. This is an example of the kind of subtlety and ambiguity that gives these kinds of dense chords their sophisticated flavor.

You may have also noticed an interesting characteristic of the 13th chords—each of them contains *every single note* of the C Major scale, just starting in a different place. This leads to our next topic...

Non-Triadic Chords

Since 9th, 11th, and 13th chords all include intervals larger than an octave, we can create closely related harmonies by simply "folding" the upper extensions down so that they're compacted into a single octave. For example, compacting our 13th chord built on C results in this:

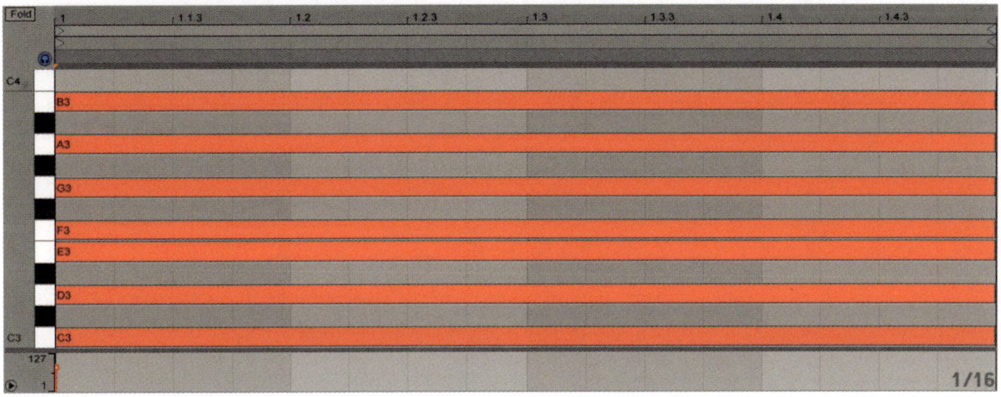

Although this contains exactly the same pitches as the original 13th, it is voiced using adjacent notes rather than every other note. Chords built on adjacent notes are called *secundal* chords or *clusters*.

Now that we know we can build chords from thirds or from seconds, it follows that we can build chords from other intervals as well. Chords built by stacking notes that are five semitones apart are known as *quartal* chords, while stacking notes seven semitones apart yields *quintal* chords. Here are examples of five-note quartal and quintal chords built from C:

As with the extended chords discussed previously, these very "wide" chords can be compacted to fit within a single octave, often resulting (again) in secundal constructions. In fact, the two chords used in the previous example form a quite nice two-chord progression when condensed in this way:

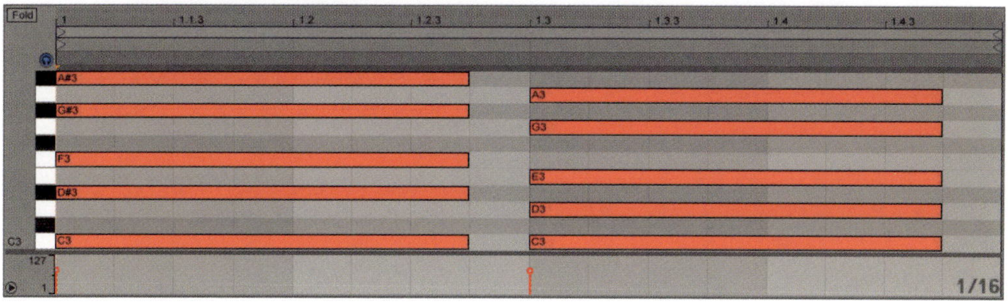

Note that these non-triadic harmonies usually aren't considered to have major or minor quality; in most contexts, they exist outside of the major/minor domain. Regardless, they are commonly used in jazz and modern classical music, again largely connected in progressions via voice leading rather than goal-oriented functionality.

This is just a sampling of the kinds of chords that are available when we expand our palette beyond conventional triads. But even using this expanded repertoire should allow you to come up with more colorful harmony than would be possible with triads alone.

A Real-World Example

The classic house track "Can You Feel It" by Mr. Fingers is a great example of some of these types of extended harmonies. The progression in the pad sound that occurs all through the track is only three chords, but they're exactly right. They also demonstrate how analysis of this type of harmony isn't always an exact science:

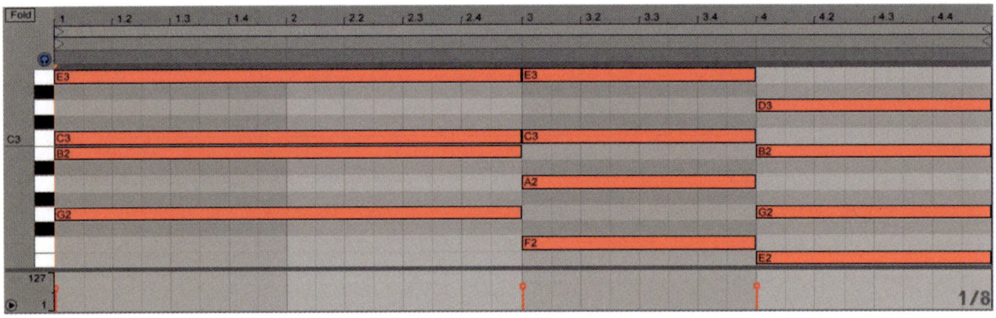

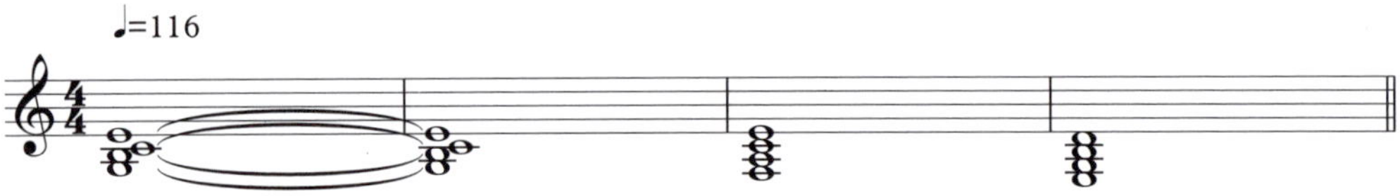

The song is in the key of A minor. So what are these chords?

1. **A minor 9:** At first glance, this labeling may seem strange. Why is this an A chord if it doesn't contain an A? The reason is the bass line, which consists of lots of repeated A and E notes underneath the harmony. Thus we have the bass line's root (A), plus the third (C), the fifth (E), seventh (G), and the ninth (B).
2. **F Major 7**: the root (F), the third, (A, both in the chord and in the bass line), the fifth (C), and the seventh (E).
3. **A minor 11**: the bass line's A, plus the fifth (E), the seventh (G), the ninth (B), and the 11th (D). Interestingly, the chord contains no third (C), which gives it an unusual, unstable color. And if we ignore the A in the bass, we could call this a simple E minor 7, which suggests a somewhat more functional progression: v - I. So is there a "right" analysis? Not really. The ambiguity is part of what makes the progression interesting.

Voice Leading and Inversions

Problem:

When you play chords on your keyboard, you find that the motion from one chord to the next sounds choppy or abrupt. Furthermore, you feel like you have to move your hands really far to get from one chord to another. But in the music that inspires you, the chords always sound like they move smoothly from one to another. What are your favorite artists doing that makes such a difference?

Creating smooth, flowing chord progressions often has less to do with what the actual chords are than it does with the nature of the *voice leading* from one chord to the next. Here's some information about how voice leading works and how to use it to create more satisfying harmony in your own music.

Solution:

Although we normally think of a chord as a vertical construction, we can think of the motion between chords as a series of horizontal constructions. That is, when one chord moves to another, the individual voices within those chords can be thought of as separate melodic lines. This relationship between the separate voices when moving between chords is known as voice leading.

Although voice leading is a big topic, we can use just a few basic voice leading principles to help create smoother, better-sounding chord progressions. In general, smooth voice leading results from *minimizing the amount of motion from one note to the next within a single voice.* This means moving the smallest possible number of semitones, as well as preserving *common tones* whenever possible. (Common tones are notes that remain unchanged from one chord to the next.)

As an example, let's imagine a two-chord progression that moves from a C minor chord to an F minor chord. The simplest way to construct such a progression is probably something like this:

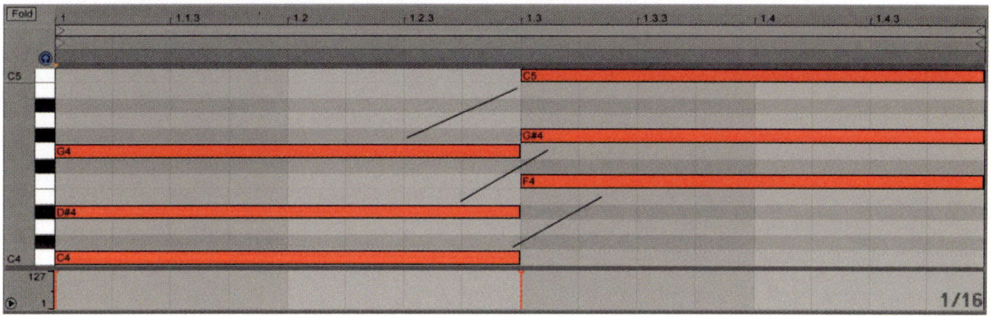

Both of these chords are in what's known as *root position*: The "roots" of the chords (C and F) are the lowest voices of the chords. For non-keyboard players root position chords are usually where the hands fall naturally. But progressions from one root position chord to another result in voice leading that's not ideal. In this example, no common tones are retained, and each voice needs to move a considerable distance (as shown by the black lines).

A smoother version of this progression might be something like this:

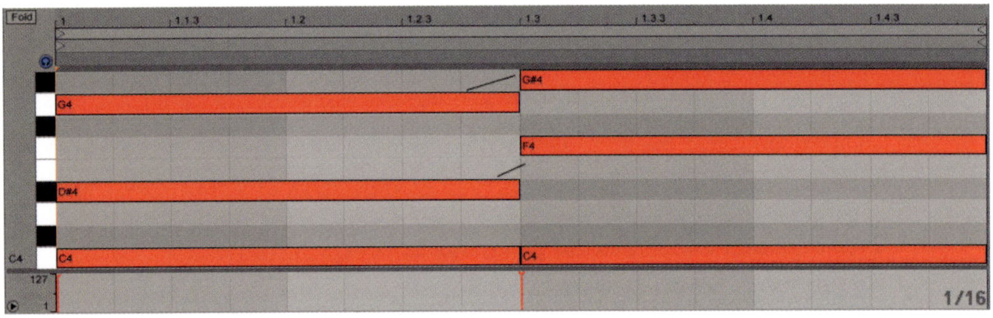

Here, the C minor chord is still in root position, but we've changed the order of the notes in the F minor chord to improve the voice leading. A reordering of a chord's notes is known as an *inversion*. In this case, we've inverted the F minor chord by placing the C (rather than the F) in the bass. This means that we maintain a common tone (the C) when moving between the chords while also decreasing the distance traveled by the upper voices.

We could achieve a similar effect by inverting the first chord while leaving the second one in root position:

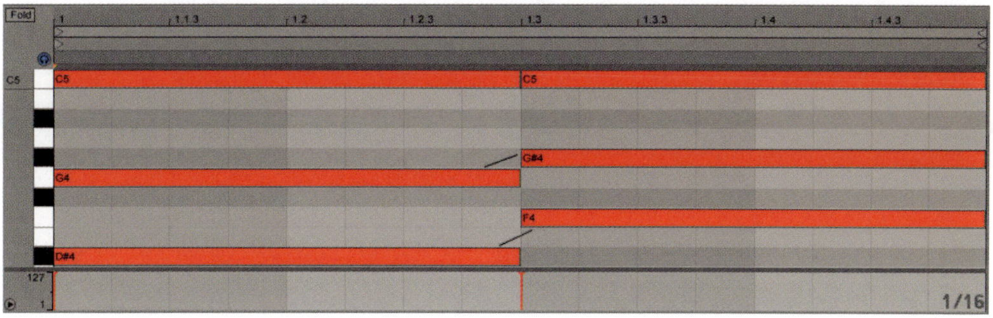

Here, we've inverted the C minor chord by placing the E♭ (rather than the C) in the bass. This means we maintain a common tone (the C) when moving between the chords, while again minimizing the distance that the other two voices travel.

By carefully using chord inversions, you can create smooth voice leading from one chord to the next, which is both easier to play and (generally) sounds better. But note that there are certain cases (as discussed in the chapter on Parallel Harmony (page 264)), when you might not want to change the voicing of chords but instead move in parallel from one chord to another. The choice depends on genre and personal taste.

Parallel Harmony

Problem:

There's a certain quality to the chord progressions in a lot of deep house, post-dubstep, and related styles that seems to be difficult to replicate in your own music.

Harmony in house music and its variants is often a tricky thing to dissect. The chord progressions are often quite repetitive but also seem strangely alien—they sound quite different from the way harmonic relationships work in any other music. Here is one way to unlock some of what's going on for use in your own music.

Solution:

A lot of house music chord progressions use a technique called *parallel harmony*, which refers to a method of moving from one chord to another in which each note moves by the same number of semitones and in the same direction. Parallel harmony is essentially what you would get if you copied a chord, pasted it somewhere else, and then transposed the copy. For example, here's a chord progression (Cm7-Fm7-Gm7-B♭m7) constructed using parallel harmony:

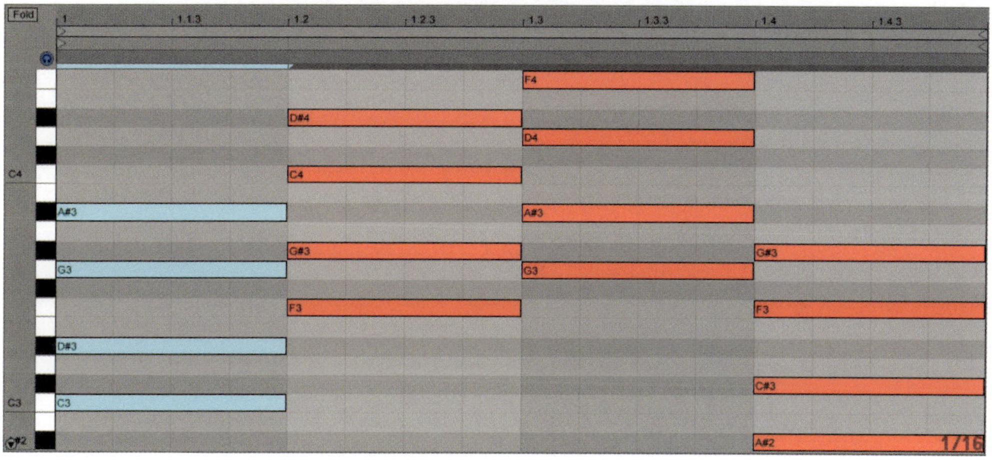

If you try to play this on a keyboard, you'll notice that you need to move your hand somewhat far to get from one chord to the next. A trained keyboard player might instead re-voice these chords to minimize hand movement, preserve notes that are shared between adjacent chords, and improve the Voice Leading (page 260).

Starting with the same voicing for the first chord, a more typical voicing of this progression might be something like:

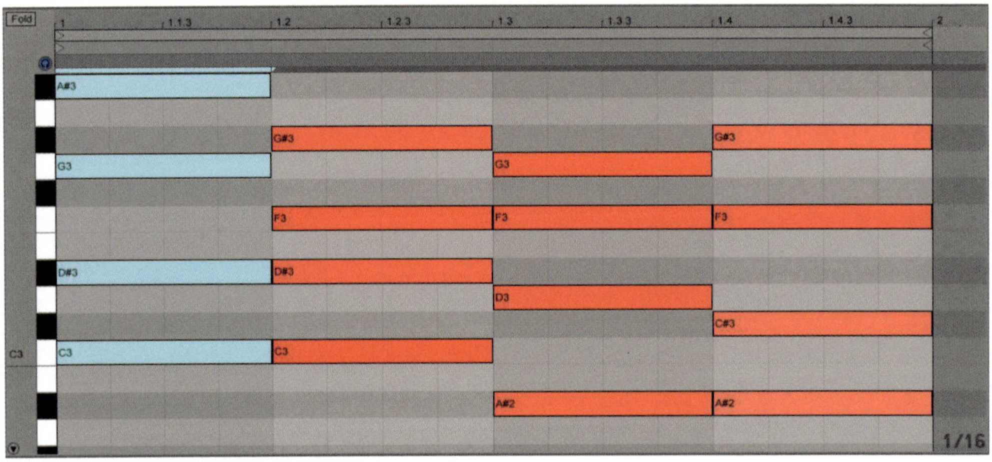

But while traditional music theory would probably call the second version "better" than the first, the parallel version has a distinct sound which has found a place in a lot of electronic music. There are a number of technical and historical reasons for this, and you can use these techniques in your own music as well:

Sampled Chords

In house music, a common technique for creating harmony is to sample a single interesting chord from another song. As with sampled breakbeats, the source for these single chords is often classic soul or jazz tracks. By then playing the sampled chord at different pitches, the resulting harmony moves in parallel.

Chord Memory

A number of classic polyphonic synths from the 80s had a feature called "chord memory," which was essentially an automatic parallel harmony generator. To use chord memory, the user would hold down a chord and press the chord memory button. After this, playing a single note on the keyboard would play the memorized chord, transposed as necessary. Many modern DAWs offer chord-generating MIDI processing tools that allow you to achieve a similar effect by automatically adding one or more notes (at specific intervals) to whichever note is played manually. This allows you to use any plug-in instrument to achieve parallel harmony.

Harmonic Rhythm

Problem:

You have a number of great-sounding chords assembled together into a great-sounding chord progression. But you can't seem to find the right speed to move from one chord to the next. You're quite happy with the rhythm of the music itself, but this doesn't seem to offer any clues for how to control the speed of the harmonic changes.

The rate at which the chords change in a piece of music is called the *harmonic rhythm*. This is a separate concept from the rhythm of individual notes and other events, which we can refer to as the *surface rhythm*. There is not necessarily any relationship between the surface rhythm and the harmonic rhythm. For example, it's certainly possible to have very active, fast surface rhythms that repeat or outline a single chord for a long time before changing to the next one.

Such a piece would have a slow harmonic rhythm. In the example below, a highly active, syncopated sixteenth-note pattern creates a fast surface rhythm. But the chords change only once per bar:

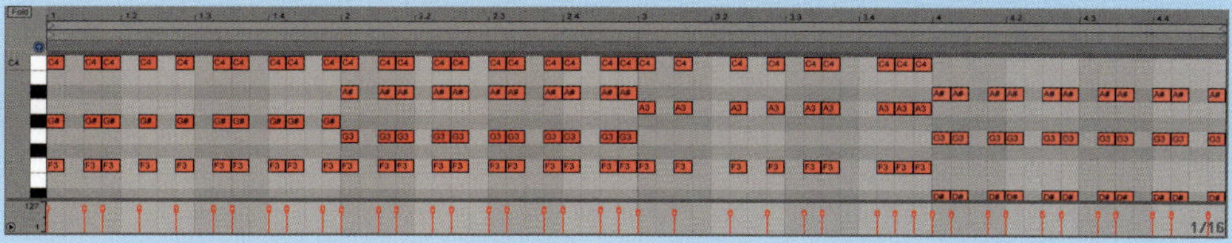

Likewise, we could have slow music but with a chord change on every note. This would likely result in a relatively fast harmonic rhythm. In the example below, the surface rhythm moves in quarter notes. But the chords also change once every quarter note. The result is a harmonic rhythm that's four times faster than the previous example but with a slower surface rhythm, resulting in a slower apparent rate of activity.

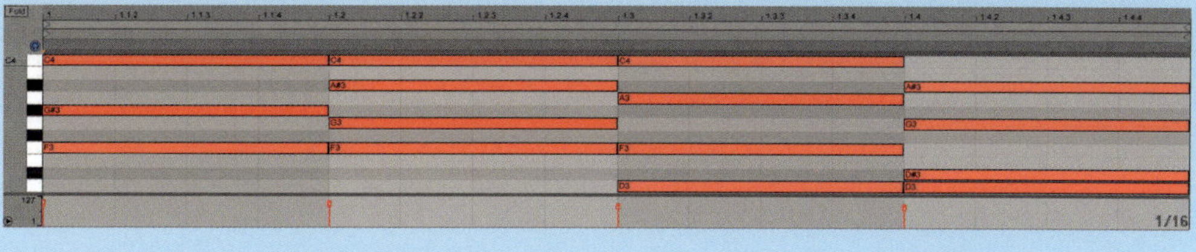

Here are some ideas for how to use harmonic rhythm in interesting ways in your own music.

Solutions:

The examples discussed earlier are actually fairly common patterns that govern the relationship between surface rhythm and harmonic rhythm. As a general (but by no means universal) rule, music with a faster surface rhythm tends to have a slower harmonic rhythm, and vice versa. For example, if the instruments that define the harmony are moving in fast notes (like sixteenths), you'll generally get good results if the harmonic rhythm moves more slowly (perhaps one chord per bar), while if those instruments are moving in slow notes (like quarters), you might consider a faster harmonic rhythm (like one chord per beat or two beats).

Another interesting way to use harmonic rhythm is to vary it to create new formal sections. For example, for your bridge or breakdown section, you might use the same basic chord progression that you used in a verse or chorus, but at half the speed. In this case, it might also be interesting to slow down the surface rhythm as well, to create a sense of anticipation before returning to the original pace when returning to the "main" sections of the track.

Conversely, you might want to think about speeding up the harmonic rhythm as a way to end the song. For example, if your last section repeats a four-bar chord progression, try condensing the same progression into two bars to give a greater sense of forward motion. (This is a variation on the ideas discussed in Short Loops as Endings (page 320).)

~ Note: Harmonic rhythm is only affected by instruments that actually contribute to the harmony. Drums and other non-pitched instruments, for example, have no relevance here. It is certainly possible to have fast rhythmic activity in the drums while also having very slow rhythmic activity in pitched instruments. In this case, you will probably only want to consider the sonic effect of the pitched instruments when thinking about your harmonic rhythm.

Repetition and Insistence

Problem:

You struggle to create bass lines, chord progressions, and melodies that work well together. But some music seems to work perfectly without any of these relationships. The notes seem almost arbitrary, and yet they always sound "right." What's happening in this music and how can you use these techniques in your own work?

How is it that some music—like house or trance—depends so heavily on harmonic relationships, while other music—like acid or minimal techno—often seems to work without any notion of harmony at all?

Solution:

Repetition can have a powerful and unexpected effect on the listener. As long as it's relatively brief, the most angular, atonal musical pattern will eventually sound completely appropriate if it's repeated persistently enough. Through regular exposure and insistence, we can't help but find patterns in chaos. As discussed in Implied Rhythm in Short Loops (page 146), you can use this perceptual illusion to find interesting rhythms in any source material, but you can also use it to create melodic patterns and bass lines.

It's common in acid techno, for example, for bass lines to be comprised of notes that are essentially arbitrary. But because these patterns are both short and endlessly repeated, they sound perfectly natural. This doesn't work for every genre—if you're writing music that's rich in harmony, with long, sustained chords supported by a bass line, it's likely that the bass notes really matter. But you'll note that in acid and minimal techno, there's often no harmony at all. This allows for more freedom in how melodies and bass lines can be constructed, and dissonance often works perfectly well in this music.

If you have access to a plug-in or instrument that can generate random sequences, try feeding a typical 303-style monophonic bass synth and see what kind of results you get. At first listen, some patterns might sound unusable. But allow yourself to listen to the pattern loop a number of times and you'll find that it will start to become musical. In principle, this will work with almost any pattern.

Of course, your ear needs to be the final judge of the results, and you're ultimately responsible for any random processes that you apply to your music (see Randomness and Responsibility (page 290)). But in many cases, you can make almost any pattern work if you're willing to repeat it with enough insistence.

The Rhythm of Automation

Problem:

You know that you can use automation to give more motion to your music, but you're not sure how to use it effectively or creatively. You end up falling back on the same standard patterns: long, smooth filter sweeps, slow, steady pitch rises, or simple adjustments to mix parameters to keep the parts in balance over the course of the arrangement. What are some ways that you can make more creative use of automation?

Automation is perhaps most commonly used to precisely sculpt a mix to ensure that levels will be perfectly balanced at all points of the song. But automation can be used for so much more than just simulating an engineer's hands on the mixer faders. Here are some ideas for using automation to add an additional layer of rhythmic interest to your music.

Solution:

Most of the time, automation is recorded in real time; the producer moves a fader or knob as the transport runs, and the motion of that control is captured as a series of points that approximates a curve that is generally smooth. The resulting automation envelope may look something like this:

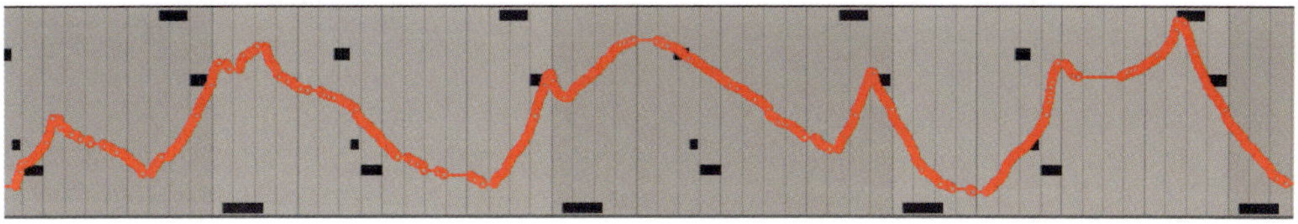

The overall shape here looks like something you'd imagine a human would make; there are occasionally somewhat "sharp" changes, but there are no *instant* ones. Also, there seems to be no real relationship between the automation envelope and either the underlying metric grid or the note events. It looks like something that was created by moving a physical control by hand.

But there's no reason why automation envelopes can't have fundamentally different properties. If automation is created by manually placing breakpoints or envelope segments at specific metric positions, the resulting envelope will have a dramatically different character. Contrast the previous example with this one:

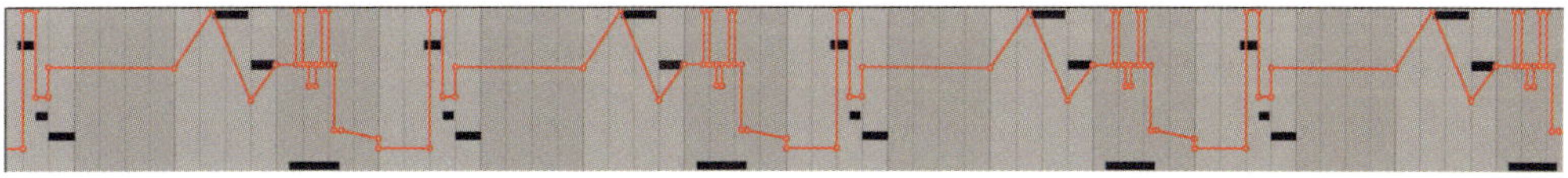

The sharp edges and instant changes look more like the waveforms used in synthesis than they do any kind of conventional parameter envelope. This is an envelope that is inherently *rhythmic*. By using envelopes like this, you can add an additional layer of activity that serves as a counterpoint to the rhythm created by the note or audio events themselves.

Rhythmic envelopes probably don't make sense for all types of parameter automation. For example, real-time recordings of parameter changes will probably work best for things like the final mix adjustments, in which you're just trying to control the relative volume balance of the various parts. But for any creative applications—synth parameters, filter or other effects settings, or even panning—you might find that you get more interesting results by using automation envelopes that are rhythmic.

Humanizing With Automation Envelopes

Problem:

When live musicians play instruments, there are subtle, constant variations in the tuning and length of notes that help to create the sense that the music is “alive.” How can you recreate this effect in electronic music?

On most traditional instruments, all or most of the stages of the amplitude envelope are entirely under the control of the performer. And on some instruments (such as woodwinds, brass instruments, and stringed instruments without frets), the player also controls the tuning of each note. But most electronic instruments use an envelope generator to determine the amplitude characteristics of the sound, and use conventional equal-tempered tuning to determine pitch. This makes these instruments predictable and easy to play, but at the expense of some of the subtlety and expression that gives non-electronic music its human character. Here are some ideas about how to use your DAW’s automation envelopes to provide some humanization to any electronic instrument.

Solution:

Most of the time, synthesizer programming involves setting the parameter values that define the sound and then mostly leaving them alone. Many producers will employ some automation to give the sound a sense of motion, but this is often applied to just a few controls—filter cutoff and maybe resonance. But by applying even subtle automation to a few more parameters, you can create much richer and more organic sounds.

Rather than treating amplitude envelope parameters as static values, try employing automation to change these values over the course of a phrase or even over your whole arrangement. In particular, by varying the attack and decay times, you can create subtle changes in the perceived duration of notes. In most cases, the actual parameter values used won't really matter much. This means you might also be able to achieve a similar effect by using parameter randomization tools (if your DAW provides them) rather than needing to create long automation envelopes. But even if you do choose to use automation, you'll likely find that this is substantially less work than editing the durations of individual MIDI notes.

Additionally, try using automation to create small variations in the overall tuning of the synth. It's critical that these changes be *extremely* small. The goal is to simulate the kinds of human intonation "errors" that give live instruments character, but tuning shifts of more than a few cents in either direction are likely to simply sound out of tune. And as with amplitude envelopes, the actual tuning values probably won't really matter, which means that you might be able to get the same effect via randomization.

By applying subtle automation or randomization to envelope and pitch parameters, you can emulate a lot of the subtle characteristics that make live instruments sound so organic. But there's no reason to stop with only these parameters. Modern synthesizers, samplers, and effects often have a huge number of adjustable parameters, many of which are either ignored outright or are set once per sound and then forgotten. Try experimenting with subtle automation changes to any of these parameters as well. You may find that the results sound artificial and strange, but it's possible that this is exactly the character your music needs.

Maximal Density

Problem:

You've completely finished the first section of a song but don't know how to go on from here. Considering how much time and effort you spent on the first part, adding a second section feels like creating an entirely new project. And since you know that there are many sections to go, the end of the song feels like it's an impossible distance away.

Moving forward with a track that's in progress can sometimes feel like an impossible task, especially if you're starting from the beginning and working your way from left to right towards the end. Here's a method for approaching the process "out of order" that may sometimes allow you to work faster.

Solution:

Instead of proceeding linearly from left to right in time, try starting with an arbitrary section in the middle of the song that is *maximally dense*; that is, a section in which every possible element that could ever happen simultaneously is actually happening simultaneously.

This song section may be purely hypothetical; by stacking every part on top of every other part you may end up with an unmusical mess which will never actually become a part of the song. If that's the case, begin subtracting elements one by one until you get to a level of density that is still high but which makes musical sense. This can then become the high point of your song.

Once you have this peak section, you can make duplicates of it and then try out various lower-density versions of the same basic material by muting or deleting various elements or tracks and auditioning the result. Each time you find a combination that you like, copy and paste it so that it becomes a new song section. The act of arranging, then, is just a matter of organizing these sections of varying density in an order that makes sense with the ebb and flow that you want for the song.

Beginning with a section of maximal density is similar to Arranging as a Subtractive Process (page 300) but is focused on the compositional stage rather than on the arranging stage. Although both ideas require that you have a pool of materials to work with, Maximal Density doesn't require you to lay them out into a song-length arrangement, but rather to stack the ideas vertically so that they comprise a single, dense section. From here, you can build your arrangement by creating variations that are texturally-reduced versions of the "master" section.

Note that this idea may only work in this very literal way if you're working in a genre such as minimal techno, in which there is not necessarily the expectation that the various song sections will be radically different from one another. In other genres in which there might be more contrast from one section to another, you may be able to take the idea of Maximal Density only so far. But even here, it can still be useful to create variations of a song part that might appear in variations throughout the song. You could even repeat the process for each section: Create a maximally dense verse, a maximally dense chorus, etc., each of which serves as the parent for smaller variations of the corresponding sections.

Deliberately Bad Listening

Problem:

The acoustics in your studio are perfect, or at least you know their imperfections well enough to account for them in your own listening. And when you listen back to your music during production, you feel like you're hearing everything there is to hear. But sometimes, when you leave the track playing and walk around for a moment, you find that the music suddenly takes on an entirely different perspective. What causes this feeling, and is there something in it that you can use to your creative advantage when composing?

Room acoustics, monitoring options, and listening positions are popular topics on the production side of electronic music-making, but there may also be things we can use (or misuse) in these areas to help us on the creative side.

Solution:

Instead of always trying to maximize the quality of your listening environment, try occasionally listening in a deliberately "bad" way. Particularly during the creation phase, doing this might help you hear things that are acoustic illusions which you might find musically interesting enough to actually incorporate into your music.

For example, rather than exclusively listening from the "sweet spot" in your studio, try regularly varying your listening position, and see what sorts of sounds emerge. Standing in the corner of your studio, for example, may dramatically change the way you perceive bass and other low-frequency components. Although you'd never want to do this when *mixing*, doing it while composing might reveal unusual bass elements (such as phantom pitches) that sound great. At this point, you'll need to take note of what these artifacts are so that you can actually create them in your song.

A more extreme version of this idea is to listen from an entirely different room—either through a wall or through a closed or open doorway. Because of the way different frequencies transmit through walls, you are likely to hear a completely different mix when listening from outside of the studio. Again, this is not a suggested way to approach mixing your track, but the artifacts and imperfections you hear as a result of this "bad" approach to listening may be compositionally useful. (Note: Obviously, if your studio is completely soundproofed then this technique won't work unless you leave the door open.)

One interesting approach when composing with headphones is to take the headphones off and turn the volume up high enough so that you can still hear the music. You will generally lose all of the mid and low frequencies when listening this way, and all that will be left is the high-frequency content. But you may hear relationships between parts (or even artifacts like phantom notes and rhythms) that are entirely absent in the music itself.

Finally, another type of "bad" listening is to turn the volume down so that the music is just barely perceptible. This can yield similar results to the headphones suggestion mentioned earlier but will generally preserve a bit more low end. However, because our ears are not equally sensitive at all frequencies, you're likely to hear certain ranges more clearly than others at low volumes, and this too may help to reveal phantom elements that might otherwise go unnoticed.

Remember—with all of these techniques, you're listening for illusions: elements of the music that aren't really there, but which are suggested by the strained or otherwise imperfect listening conditions. Once you find these (and provided you like them), you'll need to figure out how to get them into the music itself so that they can be heard by listeners in normal listening environments as well.

Randomness and Responsibility

Problem:

You have some "randomization" plug-ins that promise to create a never-ending supply of new ideas without much effort. In principle, you're excited by the potential of making lots of music with little work. But in practice, the results you're getting are unsatisfying for some reason.

There are some types of music, like classic IDM, breakcore, etc., in which constant change is a defining characteristic of the sound. Particularly with drum programming, music in these genres can be extremely time-consuming to build by hand, requiring lots of deliberately placed samples, micro-edits to parameter automation, etc. For this reason, there are a number of plug-ins and other tools available that process an incoming stream of audio and reorder it rhythmically on the fly (these often have the word "buffer" in their names or descriptions), apply effects to only specific time slices of the audio, or perform some combination of both processes.

On the other end of the musical spectrum are genres like minimal or dub techno, in which the overall rate of sonic and musical change is much slower. But even here, there are times when applying subtle randomness to some aspect of the music can kick you out of your normal patterns of production and help you find ideas that you wouldn't have found through your own deliberate action.

And when working in any genre, there may be times when you know you want something to change, but you don't care about the specific aspects of how it changes. For example, you may want the panning of a particular element to vary continuously throughout the track, but drawing in a detailed automation curve may be too time-consuming. In this case, applying some kind of randomizer to the panning may give you what you want—a continuous state of change, without the need to specify the details.

But sometimes the results just don't work. Here's a solution.

Solution:

Randomization tools can be powerful, but they lack the most important element that makes your music work—your own taste. When you're in control of every element, you're making conscious micro- and macro-level decisions about each moment of the music. If you play a wrong note (or the right note at the wrong time), you hear it immediately and fix it. But when a tool has generated this wrong note for you, it's easy to miss.

To go back to the early IDM example, consider classic tracks by artists like Squarepusher and Aphex Twin. During this era, there were no plug-ins that would accomplish the micro-editing that's happening in this music. What you're hearing is a process that was done moment by moment, by hand.

This is not to suggest that randomization tools are "cheating" or should be avoided. There's nothing inherently wrong with finding ways to eliminate unnecessary work. But it's important to keep yourself fully invested in the process. Although the secrets behind what happens in your studio are yours, in the end, your name will be on this music. Even if it's made entirely by a machine via some sort of algorithmic composition process, it is still your job to evaluate the results that are generated, discard the ones that don't work, and keep the ones that do. The less you're involved in the creative minutiae, the more you need to be involved in actively auditioning the results.

In terms of specific technical steps, try slowing things down, soloing them, or bouncing the results to audio so that you can really assess whether the randomized output has the musical effect you want. If you're working with randomizers that generate or alter MIDI data, try re-recording this output to another MIDI track so that you can capture the randomized material as "real" MIDI data, which you can then edit later. One nice way to test the limits of your randomization processes is to increase the amount of randomization until it's clearly too extreme, and then dial it back from there. The "right" amount is totally subjective and depends on the genre you're working in and, most importantly, your personal taste.

As always, you must be willing to throw material away if it doesn't sound right. Listen to—and take responsibility for—every moment.

Dramatic Arc

Problem:

You can't seem to create an arrangement that really feels like a convincing musical journey. You can put various song parts together and move them around, but nothing you do seems to create the feeling you get from listening to your favorite music. You find it very hard to create a sense of drama or tension and release. You don't understand how to structure musical time convincingly over the course of 4-10 minutes (and are amazed that a good DJ can do it over the course of hours!).

Solution:

There are many different ways to organize musical materials over time, but one of the most successful is a three-part structure called the *dramatic arc* that is also commonly used in theater, film, and other narrative or dramatic media.

The dramatic arc refers to three main sections: exposition, climax, and dénouement, which are connected by rising action at the beginning and falling action towards the end. A graphical representation of this arc (known as *Freytag's pyramid*) is below:

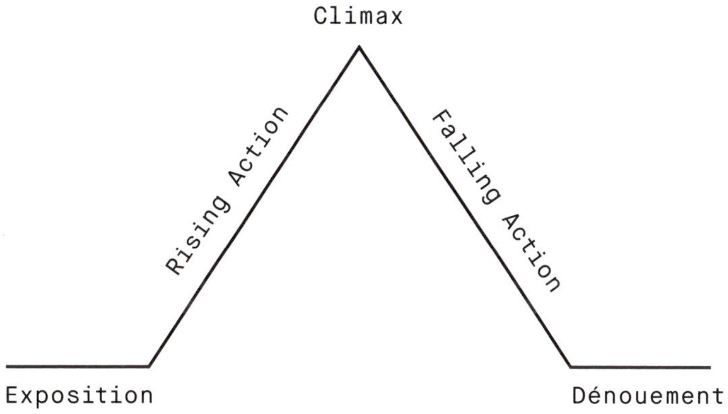

Exposition: In stories, this is the introduction of characters and the setting of the scene. In music, the exposition is the introduction of musical materials (melodies, harmonic progressions, rhythmic ideas, etc.) that will appear through the piece.

Rising action: This is the section when tension builds towards the climax. In stories, this usually means conflict between a protagonist and adversaries. In music, it might mean variations or mutations of the materials that were introduced in the exposition.

Climax: This is the peak of dramatic tension in the work. In a story, this is often the "turning point" for the protagonists, the point at which fortunes shift from bad to good or vice versa. In music, the climax is often marked by a sudden increase in textural density (e.g., "the drop" in dubstep or EDM).

Falling action: This is a section of relaxing tension after the climax. In stories, this section serves to resolve outstanding conflicts from the climax. In music, this section might mirror the activity from the rising action section.

Dénouement: In stories, the dénouement is often a mirror of the exposition, in which characters return to normalcy after the events that make up the tension of the story. In music, this might mean a restatement of established musical materials (e.g., a repeated chorus) or a gradual dissolution (e.g., a fade out into silence).

While the dramatic arc is normally thought of as a formal structure for the piece as a whole, in music it can also be used as the structure for smaller- or larger-scale components. On the micro level, a single melodic idea can be structured as a dramatic arc; consider a melody that rises to a peak before falling again to its starting pitch. (An example like this is quite literal, with a melodic contour (see Creating Melodies 1: Contour (page 212)) that visually matches the shape of Freytag's pyramid. Of course, it's also possible to build tension without literally ascending to a higher pitch.) On the macro level, a good DJ set often follows something like a dramatic arc as well, with tension building to a climax over the course of an hour or more, before resolving back to a lower energy level over a similar amount of time.

There are, of course, many types of musical forms that bear no resemblance to the conventional dramatic arc. Genres like dub or minimal techno, for example, generally have no clear build to a climax. In this music, dramatic tension is created in entirely different ways, often through careful attention to sound design and subtle changes in an otherwise static texture over time. But in some situations, using the dramatic arc as a model for musical form can work extremely well.

Problems of Finishing

Arranging as a Subtractive Process

Problem:

You have more than enough ideas to make up a finished song but don't know how to actually put the arrangement together. Even the process of arranging sounds like an intimidating commitment. How can you even begin, let alone finish?

In the context of music creation in a DAW, the arrangement refers to the layout of the parts of your song along a timeline. You may have assembled a rich pool of material, but the actual act of putting that material in some kind of order that unfolds over time is what will eventually turn that material into a finished song.

Getting from "pile of stuff" to "song" is a difficult process, both conceptually and technically. The most common way people approach creating an arrangement is the most obvious one: Gradually fill the empty arrangement with various combinations of the material you've made, moving from left (the beginning) to right (the end). In this workflow, the arrangement timeline is analogous to a blank canvas to which you apply paint until a finished painting appears from what was originally empty, white space.

This process works, of course. But facing emptiness can be scary. Even though you've already put in a considerable amount of time preparing the materials that you plan to use, you now face something that might feel like a reset to zero. Beginnings are hard, and a blank canvas (or empty timeline) can be a difficult mental bridge to cross.

Solution:

If you're finding that you're stuck at the arranging stage, here's one process that might help: Start by immediately filling your entire arrangement with material, on every track. Spend as little time as possible thinking about this step; the goal right now isn't to try to create a good arrangement. You just want to start with something rather than nothing. It's OK that you don't know how long the song will eventually be. Just fill up an average song's worth of time (or even more) in whatever way is the fastest for your particular DAW—by copy/pasting blocks of clips over and over again, via a "duplicate" command, or (in some DAWs) by dragging the right edges of clips to extend them.

Perhaps you've already given some thought to how your material will be divided. Maybe you've named certain clips things like "Verse" and "Chorus" so that you can better organize them when arranging. Don't worry about any of that for now. In fact, don't even try to use all of the material you have. Just grab a pile of ideas from each track, and fill the empty space. This process should take no more than about 20 seconds. If you're spending more time than this, it probably means you're trying to make creative decisions. For example, maybe you're thinking "I already know that this chunk of ideas will go before this chunk of ideas, so to save time later, I'll just lay them out in that order now." Resist the temptation to organize anything in this phase, and simply move as fast as possible.

As an example, here's a 6-minute arrangement timeline, filled as quickly as possible.

Now that you've filled the timeline, the process of actually making your arrangement into music becomes one of subtraction rather than addition. If the traditional arranging workflow is analogous to painting, the subtractive workflow is analogous to sculpting. You're beginning with a solid block of raw material and then gradually chipping away at it, creating space where there used to be stuff, rather than filling space that used to be empty.

This can be a much more productive way to work for a number of reasons. For example, it's often easier to hear when something is bad than it is to imagine something good. If a particular combination of ideas doesn't make musical sense, you can generally feel this right away, and the steps to fix it may be obvious: Maybe an element is simply too loud, or the bass line clashes with the harmony. And because you're listening back to an actual flow of sound over time, you'll probably have an intuitive sense of when a song section has been going on for too long—your own taste will tell you that it's time for a change.

If you're working in a genre in which textural density tends to increase and decrease as the song progresses, you may already have your "thickest" sections of material finished at this point. You may find that you're actually able to work backwards from the end of the song towards the beginning, removing more and more elements as you go back in time.

~ Bonus tip: Most DAWs provide a way to insert or delete chunks of empty time in the middle of an arrangement. When using a subtractive process, these tools can be extremely helpful. For example, you may have finished editing work on what you originally thought would be two adjacent sections of material, but then realized that something else should come in between, or that the first section needs to be twice as long. Inserting time in the middle automatically shifts everything after this point to the right, which is much faster and safer than trying to cut and paste many tracks' worth of material manually. Or maybe you've realized that a section you've been editing is too long. If your DAW has it, use the delete time command to remove the excess material, which will cause everything to the right to automatically shift to the left to fill in the gap.

The Power of Erasing

"It seems that perfection is reached not when there is nothing left to add, but when there is nothing left to take away."

– Antoine de Saint-Exupéry

Problem:

You feel like your music lacks the "fullness" of the music that inspires you. But your attempts to solve the problem often end in music that just feels cluttered or messy.

It's tempting to think of a song as being something like an unlimited physical space, and that the way to fill the space involves adding more stuff. But in reality, musical space has boundaries, like a canvas: There is a limit to how much you can add before you're simply covering something that's already there.

Solution:

On the production side of music-making, it's common to hear about "making space" for each element in your mix. Normally, this means eliminating overlapping frequencies by using EQ to carve out a band of frequencies in one instrument that you'd like to be more dominant in another. But the same process can be applied on the composition side as well (and may even save you from having to do EQ surgery afterwards).

If your music feels "small" or "weak" or "lacking power," the real solution may be to take parts away rather than to add more. It may feel counterintuitive, but the reality is that each part you add requires the others to fight that much harder for your listener's attention. Of course, this paring-down strategy only works if the parts you have are as good as they can be. But if you allow yourself to fill musical space by adding parts, you run the risk of treating each part with less care than you might otherwise, rather than really investing the time and energy into getting a few elements to be perfect.

This is *not* an argument for minimalism or for any kind of specific approach to genre. There's plenty of "minimal" music that fits that description because of factors other than textural density. Music with a slow rate of change, for example, is often heard as minimal, regardless of how many elements are happening. Likewise, plenty of maximally active and seemingly dense music (such as some commercial EDM) can still sound clear and open because of a conscious effort to limit the number of simultaneous parts. The important point is to add parts as necessary, but *only* as necessary, and to be ruthless about removing things that aren't really contributing to the music.

A sense of "fullness" can usually be created by carefully balancing just a few things. If each part is placed in its own space, both in terms of composition and production, then a song has a better chance of feeling "complete" than it does if many parts are competing for the same space.

In addition to brute-force removal of entire parts, you can often get good results by "thinning out" certain elements. Techniques for this include reducing the number of notes played by a particular instrument or shortening the decay time of sustained sounds so that they quickly get out of the way of the rest of the mix.

If you employ processes such as Arranging as a Subtractive Process (page 300) or Maximal Density (page 282), you may have inadvertently created music that suffers from problems of over-layering. In these cases, you may need to do lots of erasing in order to get back to something that makes sense for your song. This is not to suggest that those processes don't work, but rather that you'll need to be extra careful and really think about whether or not you've removed enough to keep the song musical.

Formal Skeletons

Problem:

You have all of the elements you'll need for a great song, but it seems that no matter how you put them together, the arrangement feels unsatisfying. When you listen to your favorite tracks, you never have this feeling; every part seems to last just the right amount of time, tension and release are balanced perfectly, and the song just "works" exactly as it should.

Creating successful arrangements requires having a great internal sense of proportion, an understanding of how long each song section needs to be in relation to the others. Luckily, this is a skill that can be learned, and one of the best ways to learn it is by studying and copying from great examples that already exist.

Solution:

Find a song that has a form that works and that's somehow in the same musical universe as the music you're writing. Then load that song into an empty project in your DAW, starting from the left edge (bar 1). Carefully adjust the tempo of your project so that it perfectly matches the tempo of the song you've loaded. This ensures that your DAW's beat grid will align perfectly with the actual beats in the song.

Once you have this set up, carefully listen to the song. When you hear a formal division (or even an interesting moment within a formal section), stop playback and place a marker at that point. Then continue listening from that point until you reach the next formal division, at which point you'll stop and add another marker. Continue this process until you reach the end of the song. If your DAW allows this, give the markers descriptive or functional names that will help you to understand the musical significance of the marker without having to listen again. If the song is in a genre that uses conventional song structures, you might give these markers names like "Verse," "Chorus," etc. If not, you can simply give yourself clues like "Bass starts." Here's how a song might look when you've finished this process:

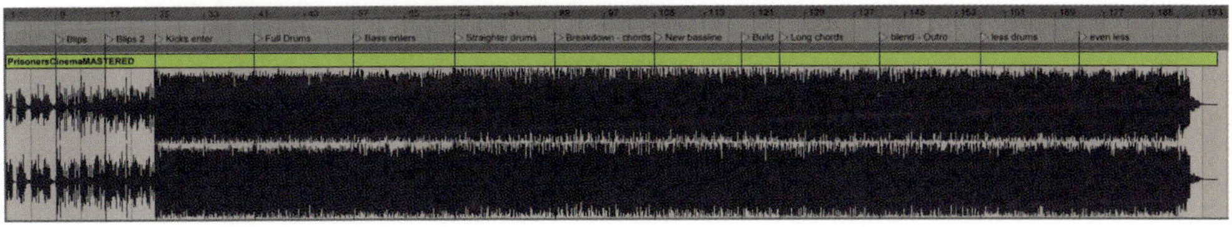

As with the above example, in most electronic genres, you'll probably find that these formal divisions will occur at multiples of four or eight bars. This is by no means universal, but it can be a handy reference when working on your own arrangements—either by nature or because it simply occurs in so much music, listeners seem to be primed to expect formal divisions at these points.

Now you can simply delete the original audio file, leaving the markers behind as a kind of skeletal outline of an arrangement that you know is effective:

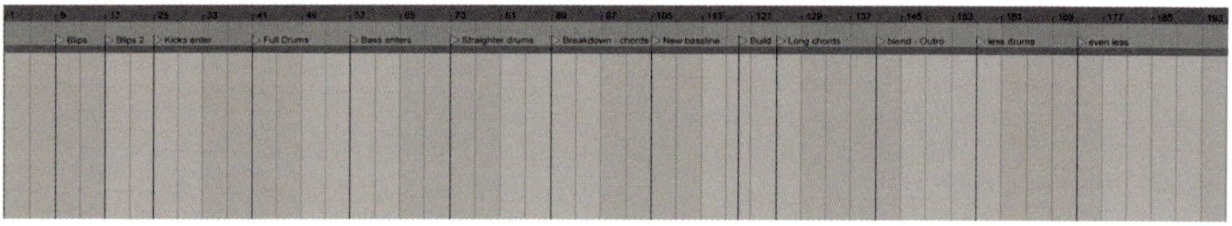

From here, you can arrange your song to fill in this formal outline. And because your materials are your own, there's little chance that you'll end up duplicating the song you've used as a reference.

~ Note: As with all of the ideas in this book, once you actually start employing this in practice, you may find that your own musical materials don't naturally fit into the arrangement skeleton perfectly. Maybe your breakdown section "wants" to be four bars longer, for example. In these cases, you must absolutely trust your instincts. The formal skeleton should be used to get you started, but you should absolutely feel free to move parts around once you're actually in the flow.

Common Forms 1: Elements of Song Form

Problem:

You have no problem creating musical ideas, but you find it difficult to organize those ideas into an arrangement that makes sense. You've heard terms like "verse," "chorus," and "bridge" to describe the sections of some songs, but you're never quite sure what these words really mean or whether or not they're relevant to your own musical work.

Understanding the various types of commonly used song sections can help your understanding of the music you hear, as well as provide options for the music you write. Here's more information about what these sections are, how they work, and how they relate to each other.

Solution:

Across many different genres, there are a handful of terms that are commonly used to refer to the various sections of a song. Much music, especially in genres that are related to pop music, is structured by combining these standard section types in a variety of ways. The most common sections are:

Verse or "A" Section: A song's verse is generally a recurring section—usually 16 or 32 bars in length—that serves as the main body of the song. In music with lyrics, the verse often tells the "story."

Chorus or "B" Section: The chorus is usually also recurring, and of comparable length to the verse. It acts as a contrast to the material of the verse and usually contains the "hook" of the song—a melodic idea that is intended to stick in the listener's head. Often, the chorus serves as a point of musical resolution, while the verse creates musical tension. Another important distinction between verse and chorus: Recurring verses share the same music but they generally have different lyrics, while recurring choruses most often share both music and lyrics. Additionally, in music with lyrics, the chorus often contains the title of the song. As a general rule, the first chorus in a song occurs after a verse (although there are some songs that begin with a chorus).

Bridge or "C" Section: The bridge serves as a contrast to both the verse and chorus and typically occurs only once in a song. Musically, bridges are often substantially different from the rest of the music in the song; they may be in a different key, employ unusual chord progressions, or have a dramatically different level of textural density and energy. In some types of music, the bridge is used for instrumental solos. Generally, the bridge occurs only after at least one verse and one chorus.

The A, B, and C letter names are often used to create formal diagrams of particular songs, and this can be a useful tool in your own Active Listening (page 30) or when writing a Catalog of Attributes (page 22). For example, one common form in commercial music is **ABABCB** or **Verse-Chorus-Verse-Chorus-Bridge-Chorus.** In some songs that use this basic form, there may be one or more additional choruses added to the end. But otherwise, this form is used unchanged in probably the majority of contemporary pop songs you'll hear on the radio. "Royals" by Lorde is an example of ABABCB form followed exactly.

Although there is a wide variety of possible song forms that can be made just from various combinations of verse, chorus, and bridge, these types of sectional constructions are less commonly used in more underground or experimental music. For example, most contemporary electronic genres without vocals tend to avoid conventional verse and chorus sections, and instead create formal contrast via addition and subtraction of layers (see Common Forms 2: Layering as Form (page 316)). But if you're working in genres more closely related to pop music, you can create a lot of music using only these few section types.

Common Forms 2: Layering as Form

Problem:

You have no problem creating musical ideas, but you find it difficult to organize those ideas into an arrangement that makes sense. You've heard terms like "buildup," "breakdown," and "drop" to describe the sections of some songs, but you're never quite sure what these words really mean or whether or not they're relevant to your own musical work.

Understanding how layering and textural density work can help your understanding of the music you hear, as well as provide options for the music you write.

Solution:

In contrast to the structure of song forms (see Common Forms 1: Elements of Song Form (page 312)), many of the more "pure" electronic genres (such as some techno, trance, dubstep, etc.) avoid the use of sectional designs altogether. Instead, a sense of form in these genres is often established by continuous variation of textural density around a relatively small amount of material—what would sometimes comprise only a single section in more pop-oriented genres.

For example, in modern genres such as American dubstep, a single basic collection of material is often used from the beginning to the end of the track. Contrast, then, is created through layering: the careful addition and subtraction of parts in order to change the density of the underlying texture. There are a handful of terms that are commonly used to refer to the various parts of a song constructed in this way. These terms include:

Buildup: A track's buildup is a section—usually 16 or 32 bars in length, or some multiple of those—in which layers are added, increasing the music's textural density and perceived sense of energy. Buildups should create a sense of drive and forward motion and should end at a high point.

Breakdown: The breakdown is a section of lower energy, designed as a contrast to the buildup, and involves either a gradual or sudden reduction in density. Breakdowns are about removing elements with the goal of creating a sense of space. Some common breakdown techniques include removing all of the drum elements or, conversely, removing everything except drums. Breakdowns are often shorter than buildups but are commonly still in increments of 8 or 16 bars.

Drop: The drop is the climax and is generally the most texturally dense passage of music in the track. The drop can occur after either a buildup or a breakdown, depending on the overall energy contour you're trying to achieve. There are generally no more than one or two drops in a single track, although there are commonly more buildups and breakdowns.

Although the musical results are radically different and significantly more subtle than in American dubstep, similar types of layering principles occur in a variety of other electronic genres as well. Consider, for example, classic dub techno tracks like those released by labels such as Chain Reaction. In most of this music, there is no sense of sectional contrast. A bass line or drum pattern that appears at the beginning of the track is likely to appear throughout the entire track, and if new material is introduced at some point, it is an addition to the surrounding material rather than a large-scale replacement of it.

Layering as a form-defining process doesn't work for every kind of music. If you're working in genres that are closely related to pop music, you will probably benefit from using the more conventional elements of song form (see Common Forms 1: Elements of Song Form (page 312)). But for many types of "classic" electronic music, using a small amount of material subjected to ever-changing levels of textural density can be enough to create a sense of structure.

Short Loops as Endings

Problem:

You have an arrangement that's almost, but not quite, finished. The form makes sense, and the pacing, tension, and release all seem to be working. The only problem is that there seems to be no way to actually end it. What can you do to close off the final section when it seems like it could just go on forever?

A common problem when working on the late stages of a track is figuring out how to actually make it come to a real conclusion. A repeating chord progression in the closing phrase of a track, for example, may simply feel "right" if extended indefinitely. Leaving a loop playing continuously is, after all, a common way to work during the production phase of a track, and it's sometimes difficult to exit the producer mindset and enter the world of the listener, who (naturally) expects a track to end at some point. If you simply stop the music, then the ending feels abrupt and rushed. But if you go on too long, you risk ruining the pacing and balance of an otherwise well-made track. Here's a suggestion for bringing a track to a real, and satisfying, ending.

Solution:

One interesting way to end a track is to isolate a loop from somewhere in the song (the closing phrase usually works well) that is somewhat shorter than the phrase itself, and then repeat this loop a set number of times as a final musical gesture. For example, if the last passage of material in your song is an eight-bar chord progression, try isolating a one- or two-bar sub-passage within this material as a closing statement. For the listener, this material will already sound familiar, since it has been previously established in the closing phrase. But by using a short snippet instead of the full passage, we can create the illusion of speeding up, or a sudden increase in forward motion that drives towards the ending.

Additionally, you may want to further reduce the size of the loop to continue this sense of acceleration into the ending. For example, our original eight-bar loop might first become two bars. Then after repeating this two bars for a little while, we might again reduce the two bars to one bar (or shorter). You will probably start to sense a natural ending point after repeating these shortened phrases a few times. If you still don't hear an obvious ending, try simply stopping the music after a fixed, even number of shortened repetitions (say 4, 8, or 16). Via trial and error, you can often come up with an ending that works.

To add even more drive to the ending, you could try adding some Unique Events (page 322) to the final shortened loops. This will increase both the apparent speed of activity as well as the textural density, while also breaking up the "purity" of the loops.

Unique Events

Problem:

You've finished an arrangement, and you're generally happy with it. It has a variety of sections, you've created Fuzzy Boundaries (page 124) between them, they all seem to last for the right amount of time, and there are contrasts and appropriate levels of tension and release. But somehow, it still sounds like "loop music"—repetitive. You can't consider it finished in this state, because it feels too predictable; it won't offer any surprises beyond the first listen.

Modern DAWs suggest a workflow that combines loops into larger arrangements, and many genres of electronic music are defined by repeating patterns. But perfectly repeated loops can become tedious after a while. Here is one technique for creating a sense of surprise within an otherwise loop-based context.

Solution:

At various points in your arrangement, insert unique events—sounds, gestures, or variations that occur only once and are never repeated. There are a few different types of unique events you can try:

> **Single *events*.** These are short samples or sounds that can be strategically placed throughout your arrangement to add a layer of unpredictability. These can be almost anything—pitched or unpitched percussion sounds, single notes or chords played on an instrument that is otherwise never heard, etc. A good source of single events is the sample library you already have. Try finding unusual samples that would otherwise be out of context for your song. Depending on where you place these events, the effect on the listener can be quite varied. For example, placing single events at or near formal boundaries can make them feel like part of a transition, while placing them at formally insignificant moments can be quite jarring and interruptive, especially if they're also placed in odd rhythmic locations that play "against" the grid of the song.

> **Single *musical gestures*.** These are short phrases or one-time alterations to otherwise consistently repeating patterns. It's common to vary a musical phrase near a formal transition, but it can be especially interesting if you also create one-time variations within the middle of a phrase. Some DAWs offer various types of note-transformation tools, which can apply processes to a selection of MIDI notes to change some or all of them in a way that maintains a relationship to the original. These tools can provide an interesting way to create one-off musical gestures.

> **Single *processing gestures*.** Consider applying dramatic, one-time changes to the effects processing on one or more tracks. For example, set up a chain of effects but leave them bypassed or off. Then use automation to make them active only once before disabling them again. Single processing gestures can be especially disruptive if they're quite short or if they occur in unusual places in a phrase.

Depending on the genre you're working in, you can be quite creative with these unique events. Unless you're working in a very commercial context, you don't generally need to worry that "weird" (i.e., out of key, out of rhythm, etc.) unique events will ruin the texture of the music. But note that you should probably use them sparingly within a single song. Even though each individual event occurs only once, using too many unique events in a song can create its own sense of predictability. Listeners will begin to expect that something jarring or unusual will occur, which reduces the effectiveness of the technique.

Three Ways to End

Problem:

You're staring at an arrangement that's working, but you see no way to come to a convincing ending.

Although endings are usually easier than beginnings, they can still be sources of considerable creative stress. After all, you've worked hard to build a strong arrangement that creates and resolves tension at the right times and in the right proportions. But all of this work could be lost if the ending doesn't "wrap up" the song in a satisfying way.

Here are three common ways to end songs.

Solutions:

1. **Mirror what you did before**. In many tracks, the work of creating the arrangement consists largely of adding and subtracting layers. Parts enter to increase the textural density and energy and then are removed to create sections of reduced energy. One way to write a satisfying conclusion is to create a mirror image of the initial "part accumulation" phase of your track. For example, if your track begins with:

> kick drum alone (8 bars)
> add other percussion (8 bars)
> add bass line (8 bars)
> add harmony and melody (8 bars),

you might then mirror this process to end the track as follows:

> remove harmony and melody (8 bars)
> remove bass line (8 bars)
> remove other percussion (8 bars)
> kick drum alone (8 bars).

2. **Loop and add/subtract**. As discussed in Short Loops as Endings (page 320), one way to end is to find a loop from somewhere in the song and simply repeat it. Insistence alone might be enough to drive the track to a convincing ending, but you can also experiment with increasing the sense of drive by adding additional layers at each loop repeat to build density and tension. On the other hand, you can also subtract or "thin out" parts at each loop repetition (possibly through the mirroring process discussed previously) in order to minimize energy and let the song end with a whimper rather than a bang. Both options work well, and the choice of which to employ depends on taste and musical context.

3. **Fade out**. Fade outs have negative connotations among electronic musicians, possibly because tracks with fades can be a bit challenging to use in the context of a DJ mix. But there are definitely situations in which a simple fade into silence is the right choice.

It's important to note the philosophical implication of the fade out: It suggests to the listener that the song might actually never end. With this in mind, it probably only makes sense to fade out if you've settled into closing material that would really work well if left looping indefinitely. Jagged, asymmetrical, or otherwise "harsh" passages probably don't make good material with which to fade out. Another important point to consider is where in the production process the fade out should be employed. If you plan to have your track mastered (or to master it yourself), it may be better to wait until the mastering stage to do the fade. This is because the sound of a mix fading can change dramatically depending on whether it happens before or after final mastering compression.

Rendering as Commitment

Problem:

You're nearly finished with the song. The arrangement is perfect, the mix is coming together, and you expect that you're just a few minor tweaks away from something you'll be really happy with. But then you start thinking "what if I could make these sounds even better?" So you go back to your synths and start tweaking knobs. One change leads to another, which leads to additional sound design work on another track, and now hours have passed and you're no closer to done—in fact, you feel like you've gone backwards, and you're just programming kick drum sounds again, like you were at the very beginning of your work on the track.

This scenario is especially common for people who work entirely in software. With total recall of every setting possible just by loading the project, we're able to easily go back and rework even the tiniest details of both the music and the sounds, regardless of what stage of the process we're at. In fact, there isn't even really a need to think in terms of "stages" anymore; we can seamlessly move between sound design, composition, arranging, and mixing right until the point at which we export the final file.

But this kind of flexibility can actually be a detriment to our real goal, which is getting music done.

Solution:

If you find that your desire to tweak the low-level details gets in the way of your ability to finish, consider adopting a workflow that simply takes away your ability to tweak. One way to do this is by rendering to audio much earlier in the process than you normally would.

Although modern DAWs blur the line between editing MIDI and audio, there is still a huge range of latent possibility (and thus distraction) available just by having access to the source instruments. By rendering to audio—and then removing the instruments that made it—you're forced to change your mode of interaction with your material. You can't change patches anymore, or adjust parameters. This forces at least the "programming synthesizers" part of the sound design process to come to an end. By closing certain doors behind you, the only way you can move is forward—writing, arranging, and mixing the song. This is essentially an Arbitrary Constraint (page 42) self-imposed for the sole purpose of eliminating possibilities.

Additionally, if you're collaborating with other people, rendering to audio streamlines project portability. It's no longer necessary for you and your collaborators to have exactly the same plug-ins, and you can be sure that shared files will open correctly on any machine. And this could also allow you to more explicitly divide up the collaborative responsibilities. For example, one of you could be entirely responsible for sound design and idea creation while the other handles arranging and mixing. By working only with rendered audio, the second person is forced to focus more on their specific roles and is unable to easily dip back into the sound design mindset.

Finally, if you're working with plug-in instruments rather than hardware ones, an additional side benefit of rendering early is that it significantly reduces your DAW's processing requirements. Working with audio is much less resource-intensive than working with virtual instruments, and constantly having to deal with an overloaded machine can itself be a damper on creativity, so working this way helps to solve this problem almost by accident.

And of course, this technique applies to more than just instruments. Including the sound of effects processing in your "early" audio renderings can be an even more extreme level of commitment. It may also help you to find new creative uses of effects, because you can be more free to capture the sound of a particular moment of processing experiments, rather than thinking of effects as locked to particular tracks. For example, you could work with an effect for a while, render the audio of its output, delete the effect, replace it with another one, and repeat.

If you own multiple DAWs, you could even consider switching between them for different stages of the production process, and rendering to audio becomes a necessary step in this case. For example, maybe you use one DAW for sound design, because you prefer the sound of some of its native instruments or effects. But you prefer another DAW for mixing because you like the look of its metering.

If you're really worried that rendering is too much of a commitment, but you still want to take advantage of the workflow benefits that rendering provides, you could try the intermediate step of saving multiple versions of your project, both pre- and post-rendering. This way, you can choose to work with the audio-only version but still go back to the older version containing the original instruments if there's a low-level change that you really need to make. The risk of working this way, however, is that any edits you make to one version will need to also be made to the other in order to keep them in sync.

Getting Feedback

Problem:

You recognize the value of feedback, but you're self-conscious about asking for other people's opinions of your music. In addition, you don't know *when* to ask for it; should you ask people to critique your in-progress tracks or only ask when things are finished (when you'll be more reluctant to make changes)? Finally, whom should you ask? Friends and family? Other producers? The anonymous internet?

Especially if you're young or new to making music, it can be difficult to have an internal sense of whether or not your work is any good. For new producers (and even for veterans), feedback from others can be helpful, but it's important to get feedback at the right time and from the right people. Here are some tips for how to improve your process of collecting feedback.

Solution:

If you're just asking for feedback because you're seeking praise, then you're not really looking to improve. The most important factor to consider when getting feedback on your creative work is whether or not you're prepared to accept criticism. And to be sure that you'll get criticism, you need to ask people who you can be sure will be honest with you. Your mother is likely to be a fan of everything you do. But unless she's also a musician, she may not be in a position to give you honest, usable feedback. Getting an ego boost can be valuable for your mental health, but beyond that it probably won't help you make better music, so be sure to consider whether or not family and friends are a good source of useful feedback or if they're instead just making you feel better.

The best people to give you constructive—and critical—feedback are probably going to be other people who are really invested in the kind of music you're trying to make: either other producers or, at least, very serious and knowledgeable fans. But even then, you need to consider the relationship between you and your critic. A teacher, for example, would probably give very different feedback to a student than that student would give to the teacher. Be careful when asking for feedback from people who are your subordinates or who might otherwise have a reason to stay on your good side. As with friends or relatives, they might just be telling you what they think you want to hear.

Getting helpful feedback from the internet can also be a challenge. Websites and forums that are made by and for music producers tend to yield feedback that is more constructive than sites that allow for truly anonymous comments (such as YouTube).

Your most valuable and astute critics, no matter how well intentioned, will probably find it difficult to objectively evaluate your music before it's finished. This is because they'll be evaluating it in comparison to tracks that are not only finished but also mastered. We naturally hear music as better even if it's just louder, and it's difficult to overcome this biological hardwiring when trying to critique music that's unfinished. One idea might be to have a "quick-and-dirty" mastering preset available that can at least get the level of an unfinished track into the general volume range of released material. This is, of course, not a substitute for real mastering. But if you're interested in getting feedback on work in progress, it will help to allow people to listen to the music without being distracted by the low volume.

Also, when asking for feedback, be sure to ask for specifics. Asking someone if they like the song will get you a yes or no answer, which isn't really of much use. But asking for details—about sounds, form, and other fine details—will likely yield much more useful feedback about your musical decisions.

Remember that once you've released something into the world—whether on a label or just on your own via the internet—you'll get criticism no matter what. You may find it beneficial to hear some of this feedback ahead of time by asking for it early. Just make sure you do it at the right time and from the right people.

Diminishing Returns

"The perfect is the enemy of the good."
— Voltaire

"Art is never finished, only abandoned."
— Leonardo da Vinci

Problem:

You regularly notice that your rate of progress gets slower and slower as you get closer to the end of the song. The beginning creation phase is very fast, and this always feels inspiring. But endings seem to take forever. You're constantly going back to refine, never quite sure that things are as good as they can be. As a result, you get increasingly discouraged as time goes on, and the final stages of work on a song are the most time-consuming and painful.

Most producers are perfectionists. We want our tracks to be better than the ones that inspire us, and at least as good as some abstract ideal that we have in the back of our mind for what our music should be. But in reality, perfection is unattainable, and continuing to tinker with a song in the very late stages may actually make things worse.

Solution:

As difficult as it might feel in the moment, it's important to learn to recognize the point at which the song is "good enough." This is not the point at which you can continue to make *real* improvements; if continuing to work is really making things better, then you should continue to work! Instead, this is the point at which continuing to work will yield meaningless or arbitrary results. Learning where this point is in the production process is different for everyone. But if you regularly find yourself endlessly tweaking what is essentially a finished mix, you've probably reached the point of diminishing returns.

Most of the time, this late-stage tweaking is the result of a fear of commitment. Once we decide that the song is finished, we might be stricken with doubt: "If I had worked harder, would it have been better?" But it's important to realize that, by this stage, you've probably already made all of the hard decisions that need to be made. At best, continuing to tweak will probably just waste time that could be better spent getting to work on the next track. In the worst case, you might actually go backwards and make the track worse. This is because your initial decisions often prove to be the right ones, and the more time you spend second-guessing yourself, the more likely you are to override your instincts in a negative way.

Although it will take time and concentration, learn to find the point where the track isn't going to benefit from further work, and train yourself to stop there. In the long run, you'll finish more music without sacrificing quality.

Fail Better

"Ever tried. Ever failed. No matter. Try again. Fail again. Fail better."
– Samuel Beckett, *Worstward Ho*

Problem:

The closer you get to finishing the track, the more you realize that it's a failure. It will be impossible to turn this into something you'll be proud of. Why bother finishing it at all? Wouldn't it make more sense to just abandon it and start over on a completely different project?

It's depressing to realize that you've made something bad. It's even more depressing to realize it while you're still working on it but after it's beyond any hope of salvation. But in this situation, there are still valid reasons to keep going and finish the track anyway.

Solution:

Most producers have started far more tracks than they've finished. It's much easier to give up in the middle of a project and move on to something new than it is to see a project through to the very end.

But what most producers don't realize is that each stage of the music-making process is itself a thing that requires practice. We get to be better sound designers by designing sounds. We get to be better drum programmers by programming drums. And we get to be better song finishers by *finishing songs*. Because of this, the more songs we start but don't finish, the more opportunities we miss out on to practice finishing. And as a result, we might continually improve at various aspects of the early stages, but we'll never improve at actually getting things done.

If you realize very early that what you're working on isn't going to be successful, you probably have time to change directions and make things better. But if you're very late in the process of making the track before realizing that it's not good, it might be too late to fix it without completely gutting it (which is essentially the same as starting over). In these cases, forcing yourself to finish—no matter how painful—is often better than giving up. You'll not only get practice finishing, but you'll also get practice failing, in itself a valuable skill to learn in a subjective and unpredictable business like art. The better you get at finishing, and the better you get at coping with failure, the better your chances will be the next time you begin (and, hopefully, finish) a project.

If the track is really as bad as you think, maybe there is a natural end point that's earlier than where you'd stop with a track you were happy with. For example, it might not make sense to get your new track professionally mastered. And it might be a good idea to not share it with the public. Maybe it just goes right back into your Scraps and Sketches (page 94) folder, to be pulled apart for use in other tracks later. But the important thing is that you actually finish the arrangement, if for no other reason than to practice, improve, and experience how it feels to finish.

Credits

Edited by Mark Garvey.
Proofread by Rose Knudsen.
Book design by Maggie Tang.

Special thanks to the following people for providing valuable feedback on early versions of this book: Savannah Agger, Gerhard Behles, Noel Bush, Michael Ford, Coleman Goughary, Ian Hobson, Alexander Joscht, Steffen Klein, Adam Mannegren, Takeshi Nishimoto, and Huston Singletary.

About the author

Dennis DeSantis is a composer, sound designer, percussionist, and the Head of Documentation for Ableton. His electronic music appears on labels such as Ghostly, Global Underground, Cocoon and Kanzleramt, and he has performed throughout North America, Europe, and Japan. Dennis has a Doctor of Musical Arts degree in Composition from the Eastman School of Music, and also has composition degrees from Yale University and Western Michigan University.

About Ableton

Ableton makes products for music makers to create, produce and perform music. These include Live, a software that combines traditional studio technologies with the freedom of working without a timeline; Push, a hardware instrument for hands-on playing and composing with Live; and Link, a technology that allows multiple devices to play in time together over a wireless connection.

Ableton was founded in 1999 by musicians in need of new creative tools. The first version of Live was released in 2001. The company is led by its founders from its headquarters in Berlin, and has additional offices in Los Angeles and Tokyo. About 300 people work at Ableton across the world.

Notes

Notes

Notes

ISBN 978-3-9817165-0-4